Leadership

in Occupational Health
and Artificial Intelligence

The UAE as a Model

Professor Doctor

Nahyan Helal

Consultant of Occupational Health
and Occupational Medicine

2025

GULF BOOK
SERVICES

GULF BOOK
SERVICES

Published by Gulf Book Services Ltd
20-22 Wenlock Road, London,
NI 7GU, UK
Email: info@gulfbooks.co.uk
Office No: G23,
Sharjah Publishing City Freezone
Sharjah – UAE

First Published by Gulf Book Services Ltd

ISBN: 978-1-917529-17-4
Year: June 2025

Why this book?

We hope that this book will be a comprehensive and simplified reference in the field of occupational health, concerned with foreseeing the future through innovation, and contribute to the establishment of work environments with Emirati specificity that reflect the quality of life and embrace occupational health and wellness in the United Arab Emirates.

Mission

Promoting occupational health and wellness in UAE work environments, enhancing the health and productivity of working individuals, and achieving safety and well-being, through innovation and technology, with a pioneering Emirati vision.

Objectives

- Provide a practical and reference roadmap to promote occupational health and wellness in UAE institutions.
- Highlight the role of artificial intelligence and automation in building advanced and secure work environments.
- Showcase applied models for occupational health and wellness programs and provide successful case studies.
- Spread awareness of the importance of occupational health as an essential element led to comprehensive quality of life and prosperity.

Introduction

In an era where the world is increasingly focused on shaping the future through automation and artificial intelligence, occupational health is emerging as a vital and fundamental pillar in developing work environments and enhancing both well-being and productivity. No longer limited to physical protection, occupational health serves as a foundation for a holistic quality of life; one that supports institutional growth and inspires creativity. Aligned with this vision, the UAE government is committed to advancing health, wellness, and quality of life in its most comprehensive sense.

This book highlights the UAE government's commitment to placing workers' health at the forefront of its national strategies. The UAE will be a model for implementing smart solutions that enable proactive risk detection and effective work environments.

"Leadership in Occupational Health and Artificial Intelligence": It is more than just a book; it is a working map that combines science, knowledge, and work, putting in the hands of decision-makers modern tools and concepts for sustainable health programs based on the latest artificial intelligence technologies and the Internet of Things.

-The book aims to be a practical guide that promotes the culture of occupational health and enhances the UAE's position as a leading country in building a healthy and safe professional future for everyone.

Presentation

Health and Wellness:
Pillar of the UAE Vision for Quality of Life and Healthcare Sustainability

The UAE embodies an ambitious vision for the future that focuses on people at the core of development and prosperity, with health, wellness, and quality of life as central pillars of its national policies. This vision reflects the wise leadership's commitment to fostering innovation and foreseeing the future, particularly in the healthcare sector, which is witnessing an unprecedented transformation driven by modern technologies and artificial intelligence.

HMC Group, founded by Prof. Dr. Nahyan, the author of this book, adopts the latest medical and artificial intelligence technologies to enhance the quality of health services and ensure the sustainability of health care, in line with the UAE's vision to achieve an integrated healthy society.

The use of artificial intelligence in diagnosis, disease prediction, and health data management reflects the country's drive to harness technology to ensure the well-being of individuals and improve the efficiency of the health system.

This book responds to this advanced vision, as it reviews innovative methodologies for occupational health and wellness in work environments, with a focus on the role of modern technologies in improving the well-being and safety of workers. Under the supervision of Professor Nahyan, one of the most prominent pioneers in this field, the book provides practical solutions and implementation tools for decision-makers and specialists to create work environments that enhance productivity, stimulate creativity, and provide a sustainable and healthy professional experience.

The book scientifically and practically addresses the challenges in occupational health, offering insights drawn from global best practices and the unique Emirati experience. It highlights holistic wellness, integrating physical, psychological, and social health to position workplaces as hubs for creativity and sustainable development.

This work is not just an academic reference, but a reflection of the UAE's vision to build a future that elevates the value of human beings and puts their well-being and health at the forefront of priorities. We hope that this book will contribute to enhancing the quality of life in work environments and supporting national trends towards a healthy and sustainable future.

Bassam Darwish, M.D.

Consultant in Health Media and Medical Development

Book Introduction

"Man is the foundation of any progress, the earth itself does not change, but the one who changes it is man." With these immortal words, our father, the late Sheikh Zayed bin Sultan Al Nahyan, may God rest his soul, painted the road map for a prosperous future. These words represent the essence of the Emirati vision, which believes that human health and well-being are at the heart of any true progress and development. Creativity and productivity can only be achieved when people are placed as core attention, empowered with care and opportunity.

The work environment in the UAE is not just a place to make profits, but a field for the growth of ambitions and the creation of dreams, where the worker is valued as a human being, and embraced as an essential individual in achieving collective goals. Here, the interest in occupational health and well-being becomes not just an organizational concept, but an integral part of the spirit of this generous country, and an extension of its historical legacy rich in human values. It is a belief that care and concern for human beings are the motivation that revives and develops societies.

As His Highness Sheikh Mohamed bin Zayed Al Nahyan, President of the United Arab Emirates, said: "We seek to make the UAE at the forefront of countries that provide a healthy and comfortable work environment, to stimulate innovation and creativity in all fields." These words reflect the leadership's commitment to creating a work environment where ideas thrive, and potential is fully unleashed. It is an environment where health and well-being become drivers of creativity, transforming workplaces into true platforms for innovation and progress. Supported by modern technologies and artificial intelligence, this vision ensures the quality and sustainability of health services, aiming to build a fully integrated and healthy society.

We present this book as a knowledge tributary that reflects the UAE's philosophy of investing in people, building hope and creating a brighter future.

Health in the vision of leadership is not just a goal; it is a way of life and a future strategy. As His Highness Sheikh Mohammed bin Rashid Al Maktoum, Vice President, Prime Minister of the UAE and Ruler of Dubai, emphasized: "Health is priceless, and it is the foundation of happiness and success."

Caring for the health and well-being of workers is not just about improving performance and increasing productivity. It is part of the philosophy of daily life, where work becomes a source of inspiration and happiness, not just a burden. Therefore, occupational health and well-being is not only a human duty but a societal responsibility towards our real wealth – the human being.

A comfortable and caring work environment sustains development while reinforcing an individual's sense of worth and their ability to contribute to a brighter future. A future in which the human being, as our leadership intended, remains at the heart of every aspiration, the basis of all progress, and an inexhaustible source of hope.

Prof. Dr. Nahyan Al- Marri

Passion for occupational health, artificial intelligence, and awareness

Index

17 .... **Chapter One:** Introduction to Occupational Health and Wellness, which includes:
- Definition of occupational health and wellness and their role in quality of life.
- The importance of occupational health and its impact on individuals, institutions, and society.

39 .... **Chapter Two:** Origin and History of Occupational Health
- The historical roots of occupational health since the Industrial Revolution.
- The development of occupational health in the UAE and the role of leadership in supporting it.
- The philosophy of occupational health and the importance of prevention as a pillar.
- Scientific developments in occupational health with a focus on psychology and epidemiology.

45 .... **Chapter Three:** Challenges and Opportunities in Occupational Health and Wellness
- Occupational challenges (chemical, biological, and physical hazards).
- Psychological and social challenges and the impact of pressure and stress.
- The role of modern technology (artificial intelligence and the Internet of Things).
- The impact of legislation and policies in supporting occupational health.

49 .... **Chapter Four:** The Role of Institutions in Promoting Occupational Health and Wellness
- Responsibilities of institutions in providing safe work environments.
- Occupational health programs and their impact on public health and productivity.
- Improve performance and reduce occupational accidents.

81 .... **Chapter Five:** Improving Occupational Health and Wellbeing in the UAE
- A review of the current situation and related legislation.
- ADNOC's role as a leading model in occupational health.
- UAE-specific challenges and development opportunities (climatic factors, cultural diversity).
- Education, training, and intersectoral cooperation programmes.

119 .... **Chapter Six:** Practical strategies to improve occupational health In the UAE
- Innovation and technology in risk analysis and artificial intelligence solutions.
- Recommendations for updating national policies.
- Performance indicators and measuring the effectiveness of programs.

147 .... **Chapter Seven:** Case Studies and Recommendations
- Practical examples from the UAE and leading countries.
- Benefits of practical application of occupational health and increased awareness.
- Launching a roadmap for occupational health workers.
- The impact of applying best practices on productivity and safety.

168 .... **Sources and references**

170 .... **Features of the experience of Prof. Dr. Nahyan Al-Marri**
- Provide glimpses of Prof. Dr. Nahyan Al Marri's personal experience and his pioneering role in this field, and the success of Holistic Medical Center as the first occupational health project in the country.
By Prof. Dr. Mohammed Al-Sadiq Al-Haj Ahmed

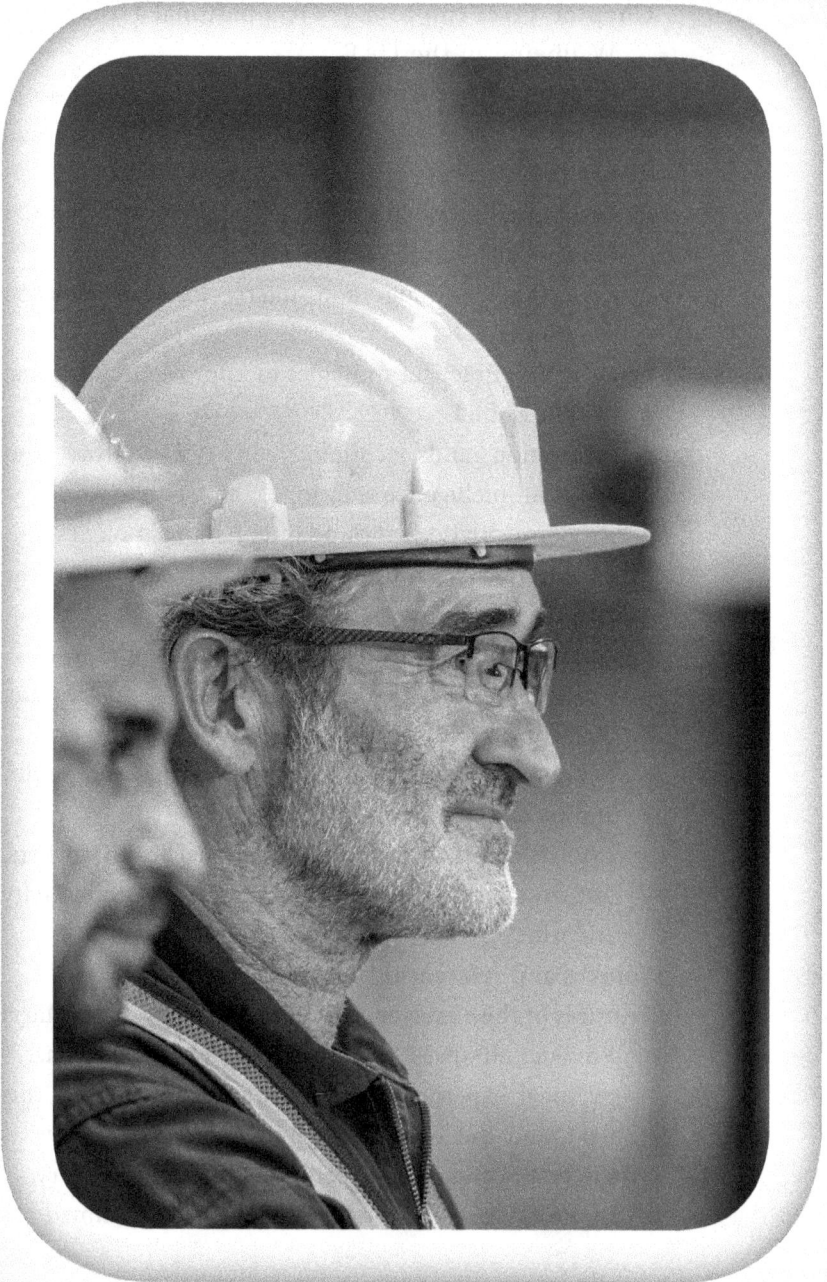

Chapter One

Introduction to Occupational Health, Wellness, and Quality of Life

Occupational Health:
Definition and pivotal role in work environments

Occupational health focuses on protecting the health and safety of workers across various work environments. It aims to create safe and healthy work environments by identifying and managing potential risks, in order to achieve the highest levels of well-being and prevent work-related illnesses and injuries. However, its scope extends beyond physical safety to encompass psychosocial well-being, boosting employee satisfaction and strengthening their connection to the workplace.

Ensuring a healthy work environment is a shared responsibility between institutions and governments, requiring attention to both the physical and psychological needs of workers. This philosophy addresses occupational health and safety care not merely as legal compliance, but as a commitment to enhancing the quality of life and fostering a positive, supportive workplace culture.

Towards a holistic vision of public health

Occupational health in the workplace is a broader concept that extends to physical, mental, and social health, aiming to improve the overall quality of life of employees by encouraging them to adopt healthy lifestyles, such as proper nutrition, exercise, and stress management. This enhances their ability to meet business challenges, contributing to improved performance and productivity.

Health is vital to creating a positive work environment, where employees feel supported and valued. Therefore, wellness in modern work environments goes beyond simply offering healthy programs to build an inclusive culture aimed at improving the balance between personal and professional life.

United Arab Emirates:
Occupational health is a strategic goal

The UAE prioritizes the health and well-being of individuals in all its sectors and has made this part of its national strategy. Within its Vision 2021-2071, the UAE has set an ambitious agenda that includes supporting public health and enhancing the quality of life. The concept of "quality of life" is one of the strategic goals that the country seeks to achieve, as it has developed many programs and policies to promote well-being.

The UAE has launched various initiatives aimed at promoting the health of workers and providing a supportive environment for health. This includes occupational health strategies, developing mental health support programs for employees, and providing universal health insurance. The UAE also collaborates with government and private institutions to encourage positive work environments, achieving its goals of building a balanced and prosperous society.

Impact of occupational health and wellness On individuals' quality of life

Occupational health and wellness play an important role in improving the quality of life of employees, reducing stress levels, increasing job satisfaction, and enhancing the sense of belonging to the organization (loyalty). Employees who feel supported by their organizations and work environment are more engaged, focused, and creative, which reflects positively on their performance.

Commitment to occupational health and wellness standards reflects the organization's appreciation of its employees and contributes to building a positive culture focused on the well-being of individuals, which is key to long-term organizational success.

International Models In Adopting Occupational Health and Wellness

Canada is one of the leading countries in the field of occupational health, having adopted programs such as the National Mental Health in the Workplace Program, which aims to support the mental health of workers in work environments. In Singapore, the 'Wellness at Work' program offers workshops focusing on stress management, healthy nutrition, and physical activity.

In these examples, organizations are not content with applying traditional occupational health standards but also seeking to build an inclusive environment that adopts a wellness approach in every aspect of the business. These programs are a model that other organizations, both in the UAE and abroad, can use to develop comprehensive health strategies.

Positive impact on institutional performance

Occupational health and wellness programs contribute to improving organizational performance by reducing the number of days of absence resulting from illness or injury and reducing costs resulting from accidents. In addition, a healthy work environment stimulates employee loyalty and morale, which drives them to commit to performing their duties effectively and motivates them to innovate to achieve organizational goals.

Occupational health and wellness in society

Occupational health and wellness are not just workplace concepts, but vital factors that directly affect the well-being and individuals' quality of life, and the sustainability of societies' development. The work environment is an extension of daily human life, where individuals spend most of their time. Thus, promoting occupational health and wellness within work environments is not limited to benefiting individuals only, but also extends to family and society at large.

Occupational health aims to reduce work-related risks, ensuring employee safety, and promoting awareness of the importance of preventing occupational accidents and work-related diseases. On the other hand, wellness focuses on psychological and social aspects, helping employees achieve a healthy balance between their professional and personal lives.

The impact of occupational health and wellness on society

1. Enhance & improve economic productivity

When organizations allocate resources to support the health of their employees, they directly contribute to improving productivity. Employees with good health and mental wellness are more efficient and able to innovate, which reflects positively on institutional performance and the national economy.

2. Reduce the health burden on society

Investing in occupational health reduces the incidence of chronic diseases and work-related injuries, reducing the burden on national healthcare systems. This means reducing the costs of treatment and prevention, thereby directing resources towards other community-based initiatives.

3. Promote social cohesion

A healthy work environment contributes to building positive relationships between employees, which leads to reduced tensions and enhanced teamwork spirit. This spirit in turn is transmitted to society, where individuals become better able to contribute to building supportive social networks.

4. Create conscious generations and a more sustainable society

Employees who live in supportive work environments pass on the values of health and wellness to their family and friends. This impact extends to future generations, creating a society more aware of health and sustainability issues.

5. Reduce health gaps

Occupational health is not exclusive to certain categories of employees. When organizations are committed to providing health programs for all, they contribute to reducing health gaps between different groups and promoting health equity in society.

Occupational Health The basis of sustainable development

Sustainable development cannot be achieved without a focus on the health and well-being of individuals. Occupational health is an essential aspect of achieving the Sustainable Development Goals, as it leads to improving the quality of life and reducing poverty by creating work environments that support people and promote their effective participation in society.

Occupational health and wellness are not just tools to improve employees' lives, they are foundational to build healthy, productive, and future ready societies. A society that values these principles fosters sustainability, resilience, and overall, well-being. By creating supportive work environments, we spark a positive impact that extends beyond the workplace and into every corner of daily life.

A healthy workforce contributes more actively to community life, strengthening social cohesion and driving civic participation. When individuals feel supported in their work environments, physically, mentally, and socially, they are more motivated, engaged, and empowered to make meaningful decisions.

At the same time, occupational health and wellness help reduce the strain on the healthcare systems by lowering the incidence of chronic illness and traumatic workplace injuries. Organizations that adopt wellness programs not only protect their employees but also promote healthier lifestyles, shaping a community culture that values wellbeing and shared responsibility.

Examples of occupational health and wellness practices in work environments

1. Occupational Safety Programs

Such initiatives include preventive measures such as providing protective clothing, training staff on safety procedures, and ensuring access to first aid. These programs help reduce occupational accidents and contribute to a safer work environment, decreasing injuries and enhancing workers' sense of safety.

2. Wellness Programs

Wellness programs include workshops on healthy nutrition, exercise, relaxation, and stress management sessions, and ongoing health counseling. Some programs also include periodic health check-ups to assess the health status of workers.

3. Achieve work-life balance

Some organizations provide flexible working options, such as working from home, reducing long working hours, and supporting personal-professional balance practices, which enhance employee satisfaction and reduce burnout rates.

Occupational Health and Wellness: Challenges in the implementation of Occupational Health and Wellness:

Despite the benefits of occupational health and wellness, their application faces some challenges:

1. **Cost:** Occupational health and wellness programs require financial investments, such as specialized facilities machines and equipment's, safety programs, and the costs of managing wellness programs.

2. **Implementation:** Some sectors face difficulty in adhering to wellness programs, due to the nature of their work.

3. **Awareness:** Promoting occupational health and wellness requires spreading awareness about its importance to achieve employee commitment.

Examples of challenges and how to overcome them

The occupational health sector is facing increasing challenges, such as digital stress resulting from the intensive use of technology, as well as occupational burnout resulting from long working hours. Possible solutions include:

- **Stress Training:** Organizations provide stress management training to workers to help them deal with daily stress.

- **Provide regular breaks:** Encouraging workers to take short breaks helps them recharge.

Work-life balance
In Future Business Environments

In future business environments, advances in artificial intelligence and the Internet of things will play a key role in supporting occupational health and wellness. These technologies can analyze health data in real time to identify optimal break times and provide personalized recommendations for maintaining employee wellbeing.

Occupational technology and health

Technology is used in many enterprises to monitor the state of health workers and predict possible risks. Smart sensors and wearables allow the collection of data on the health status of workers, such as the level of stress, allowing organizations to take proactive measures.

Occupational health during crises:

Challenges and solutions

Crises, whether natural, such as earthquakes and floods; health related like epidemics; or economic and political, pose significant challenges to societies at large and to the labor sector in particular. In such circumstances, occupational health becomes a critical factor to ensure employee safety and productivity sustainability. During times of crisis, occupational health is not just a preventive measure, it becomes vital for ensuring business continuity and safeguarding lives.

As an example of the role and importance of occupational health in protecting society in the United States, the rate of work-related injuries in 2020 treated in emergency departments was estimated at 127 per 10,000 full-time equivalent workers.

Injuries from contact with objects and equipment in 2020 were estimated at 196,000, some of which were so serious that they led to a period of interruption of work; an estimated 1.8 million workers developed work-related injuries and were treated in emergency departments during 2020.

Male workers account for about 66% of work injuries treated in emergency departments.

The three main causes of work injuries treated in emergency departments were contact with objects and equipment, stress and physical reaction, falls, slips, and stumbles without falling.

Slips, stumbles and falls represent triples account for more than a third of all injuries. Improper handling of items was the most common cause of injuries that resulted in absences from work for more than seven days. Upper limb injuries account for 50% of workplace injuries.

Occupational safety and health are an essential aspect of decent work, defined in the eighth goal of the United Nations Sustainable Development Goals (SDGs), as safe work, implying that all workers must be safe in the workplace, and not exposed to unnecessary hazards.

The 2030 Agenda for Sustainable Development Goals (SDGs) is a global call to action to eradicate poverty, protect the planet and promote sustainable development everywhere, and it is summarized in 17 goals adopted by all UN Member States in 2015.

Efforts to develop occupational health globally have also included global initiatives, such as the Vision Zero Fund, sponsored by the Group of Seven, endorsed by the G20, funded by the European

Union, the United States and others, and implemented under the ILO's flagship program Safety + Health for All".

Vision Zero unites governments, employers' organizations, workers, businesses, and other stakeholders in a shared commitment to eliminate serious and fatal occupational accidents, injuries and diseases across global supply chains.

Despite the high attention, many workers are still exposed to undue risks in their workplaces, work accidents are still common, and many work-related risk factors are left unchecked, leading to occupational injuries that could have been prevented.

During the COVID-19 pandemic, occupational health and safety have taken on greater value. The pandemic underscored the vital role of essential services such as healthcare providers, cleaners, food supply staff, and delivery personnel who faced severe risk of exposure to the virus. Their vulnerability highlighted significant safety shortcomings in many workplaces, revealing broader implications for society as a whole. In response to the pandemic, new working arrangements emerged, including the widespread adoption of remote work to help slow the virus's spread.

This unprecedented situation highlighted the need to ensure occupational safety and health for all workers, including remote workers.

Growing attention in the economic value of occupational health interventions driven from limited resource allocation and the recognition that demonstrated financial benefits make such measures more appealing to employers.

Data from a recent survey of 500 organizations found that 73% of employers believe that occupational safety and health requirements benefit their business, while 64% reported that they save money in the long run.

While safety initiatives can be effective, they do not always yield immediate financial returns. Therefore, understanding the economics of occupational safety and health interventions is essential, providing valuable input for informed decision making.

The Health Economic Assessment seeks to clearly identify, measure and evaluate all relevant cost and benefit criteria, and aims to inform decision-makers of circumstances in which indirect costs exceed the direct costs and benefits (cost-effectiveness) of the different intervention options available.

Concepts and definitions:

The old saying that "an ounce of prevention is worth a quintal of cure – quintal= 100 KG- " applies to workplace accidents. It is much better to prevent an adverse event than to try to repair the damage after it has already occurred.

While it is impossible for employers to predict every incident, it is their duty to anticipate accidents and put in place control measures to prevent them or minimize the damage they cause. They have a legal obligation to comply with laws, standard practices and safety observations to avoid emergencies and accidents.

According to (ILO - 2022) any disability or death caused by a work accident is considered a work injury, and it is different from an occupational disease, which is caused by exposure during a period due to risk factors arising from work or activity.

An occupational accident is an unexpected and unplanned event, including acts of violence, arising out of or in connection with work, resulting in one or more workers suffering personal injury, disability or death.

An occupational injury is a condition in which one worker is injured due to a single work accident. It can be fatal (where death occurs within one year of the accident) or non-fatal, with lost working time.

An accident is an unintentional event. In most cases, the term is specifically used to refer to adverse events that occurred unintentionally.

Accidents that occur in the workplace are referred to as occupational accidents. Workplace accidents include events that damage property, prevent a particular job in the workplace, or cause harm to a person present in the workplace.

Occupational accidents are also referred to as work-related accidents, and the personal harm they cause is referred to as "occupational injury", "occupational death" or any other designation that determines that the cause of the damage was occupational in nature.

There are no international standards for determining what is considered and what is not considered a professional accident.

A hazard is anything that causes injury, ill health, or damage to the property or environment.

Health and safety risks are present in every workplace. Some can be easily identified and corrected, while others represent necessary risks to the job and must be managed in other ways (for example, using protective equipment).

Most occupational hazards are inactive or have a low probability of occurring; however, employers must be prepared to deal with them because a risk that becomes active can generate an emergency.

Risks can be classified as follows:

- **Physical hazards:** These are the most common hazards and include extreme temperatures, ionizing or non-ionizing radiation, excessive noise, electricity exposure, working from heights, and unguarded machinery.
- **Mechanical hazards:** These hazards are usually created by machinery, often with protruding and moving parts.
- **Chemical hazards:** They appear when a worker is exposed to chemicals in the workplace. Some are safer than others, but for workers who are more sensitive to chemicals, even common solutions can cause illness, skin irritation or breathing problems.
- **Biological hazards:** These include viruses, bacteria, fungi, parasites and any living organism that can infect humans or transmit diseases to them.
- **Convenient hazards:** Includes considerations of the total physiological requirements of the job on the worker, beyond productivity, health and safety.
- **Psychosocial risks:** These risks may arise from a variety of psychosocial factors that workers may find unsatisfactory or frustrating.

Accidents that do not cause harm to anyone but have the potential to do so are referred to as "imminent accidents." It is a condition that can lead to injuries or deaths.

For the purposes of safety statistics, accidents causing harm or imminent accidents are sometimes grouped together as a single category. This is because the outcome of the accident is often a matter of luck.

A job site with many imminent accidents due to an object falling may be as dangerous as a job site where a falling object eventually kills someone.

It is more useful to consider the nature of the incident itself by ensuring that all incidents are reported, even if they do not result in damage.

The importance of occupational health during crises

Crises often expose employees to health and physical risks. Ensuring a safe working environment means minimizing injuries and preserving workers' lives.

1. Business continuity and production

Occupational health, supported by effective contingency plans, contributes to reducing work interruptions, helping organizations to overcome crises without significant losses.

2. Boost confidence and productivity

Demonstrating commitment to employee health and safety enhances their loyalty and trust in the organization, leading to morale and productivity even in the most difficult circumstances.

Challenges to occupational health during crises

1. Lack of resources and capabilities

Often, institutions face a lack of health equipment and capabilities to deal with crises, especially at times when the demand for these resources is high.

2. Poor planning

The absence of well-thought-out contingency plans leads to disorganized reactions that further complicate the crisis.

3. Psycho-emotional stress

Crises put huge psychological pressure on employees, leading to psychological problems such as anxiety and depression, along with physical effects.

4. Changes in the work environment

The shift from traditional work environments to remote work or work in hazardous locations poses new occupational health challenges.

The most prominent solutions to promote occupational health during crises

1. **Developing health contingency plans**
- Preparing comprehensive plans that include risk assessment, prevention measures, and mechanisms for dealing with injuries.
- Training staff on these plans to ensure an effective response to crises.

2. **Providing personal safety equipment**
- Providing employees with the necessary tools and equipment to protect them in hazardous work sites or while dealing with health crises such as epidemics.

3. **Promoting mental health**
- Establishing psychological support channels for workers to help them deal with psychological pressures.
- Organizing awareness sessions and workshops to enhance the ability to adapt to crises.

4. **Improving communication and contact channels**
- Maintaining effective communication channels with employees to provide guidance and updates clearly.
- Encouraging a culture of transparency to enhance trust between management and employees.

5. **Leveraging technology**
- Adopting digital solutions to monitor the health of employees, especially during pandemics.
- Using distance training platforms to ensure continuity of learning and awareness.

Occupational Health and the COVID-19 Crisis:
Model for learning

The COVID-19 crisis – was a real test of occupational health across the world. Organizations that invested in contingency plans, provided PPE, and adopted technology such as remote work, were able to manipulate the crisis with minimal damage.

Occupational health during crises is not a luxury but a necessity to ensure employee safety and business continuity. Organizations that prioritize the health of their employees demonstrate their ability to adapt and withstand crises. Promoting occupational health is not only a moral imperative but an investment that benefits both institutions and communities.

In the end, crises teach us that human health is the foundation on which everything is built. Therefore, it is imperative to promote occupational health to always be ready to face any new challenge.

The COVID-19 pandemic has impacted occupational health, as safety requires new measures including social distancing and hygiene standards. In the UAE, organizations have adopted measures to work remotely and implemented preventive measures such as taking temperatures and regularly disinfecting offices.

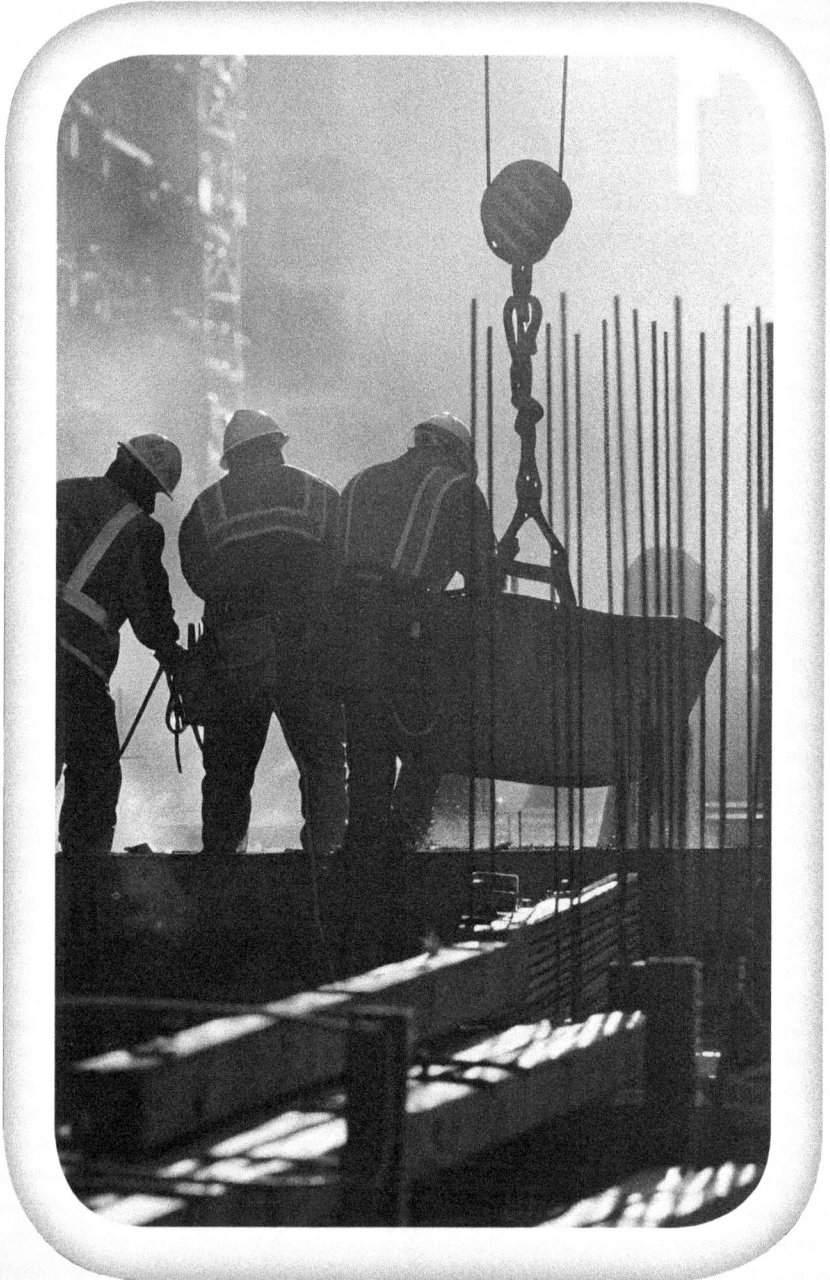

Chapter Two

Origin and history of occupational health

Occupational health and wellness represent a journey of continuous evolution towards improving work environments, from simple initiatives in ancient times to modern health programs. This history underscores the importance of collaboration between governments and institutions to achieve safe and sustainable work environments that enhance the well-being of future generations.

The history of occupational health is marked by significant shifts and developments that have shaped it into a central pillar for ensuring workers' safety and wellbeing. Over time, the concept has evolved from basic injury prevention to comprehensive systems of regulations and legislation that place workers' health and safety at the forefront. In this chapter, we will explore the historical evolution of occupational health, highlight key milestones in its development, and present documented examples, studies, and procedures that have contributed to its progress.

The concept of occupational health in ancient times

Since ancient times, there has been a primitive realization of the importance of protecting workers, especially in major civilizations such as ancient Egypt and Babylon. For example, some primitive safety rules were put in place in ancient Egypt to protect workers working on pyramid and temple construction projects. They wore simple protective clothing and used tools to help them avoid injuries.

In Babylon, civilization knew labor laws aimed at protecting workers' rights, but they were limited laws that focused mainly on regulating working hours and wages. Although this early interest was primitive, it marks the beginning of the concept of occupational health and shows the keenness of ancient societies to create as safe a working environment as possible.

Middle Ages and the emergence of handicrafts

With the arrival of the Middle Ages, people became increasingly aware of the importance of protecting workers in handicrafts such as blacksmiths and carving. Artisans were aware of the risks associated with their professions and adopted simple measures to protect themselves, but they were individual initiatives and not formally organized. These efforts are focused on the use of specific tools that reduce risk exposure and provide somewhat safer workplaces.

Although there was no formal legislation in this period, it helped raise awareness about the importance of protecting workers and implementing practices that contribute to their safety.

The Industrial Revolution and the Transformation of Work Nature

With the Industrial Revolution in the eighteenth century, the nature of work changed radically, as factories and heavy equipment appeared, and the rate of accidents and injuries increased as a result of harsh working conditions. Working environments in the factories were very dangerous, with workers working long hours in unsafe and risky environments.

This situation led to the emergence of workers' movements that began to demand better working conditions and protection of workers' rights. In Britain, legislative shifts began with the passage of the first Labour laws such as the Factories Act of 1833, which restricted working hours for children and required factories to provide certain safety standards. This law is considered one of the first legislations that established the concept of occupational health in the industrial era.

The development of health legislation in the nineteenth century

In the nineteenth century, awareness of the need to protect workers from occupational hazards began to grow, prompting governments to introduce laws aimed at protecting workers' rights and ensuring their safety. For example, in the United States, the Injured Workers Compensation Movement emerged to provide financial compensation to workers suffering work-related injuries. This movement played a key role in raising awareness about the importance of compensating injured workers and motivated institutions to adopt preventive safety measures.

In Europe, trade unions have contributed significantly to improving working conditions and pushing governments to adopt legislation to ensure worker safety. For example, the German Association for Occupational Health was founded in Germany to support workers working in factories and mines, and its efforts contributed to the German government's development of health standards aimed at protecting workers.

Occupational Health and Wellness in the Twentieth Century

At the beginning of the twentieth century, the concept of occupational health expanded to include aspects of mental health and the wellness of workers. Organizations recognized the importance of improving work environments and reducing employee stress levels, as companies began to adopt programs that comprehensively supported the health of workers. For example, some American companies in the thirties offered programs to support workers by providing health and psychological counseling and regular check-ups.

In 1950, the ILO and the World Health Organization issued a common definition of occupational health as "promoting the physical, mental and social health of workers." This definition was an important step in promoting the concept of occupational health as a fundamental right of workers.

Examples of the evolution of international legislation

The United States and the United Kingdom are leaders in occupational health, with strict laws aimed at protecting workers. In the United States, the Occupational Safety and Health Administration (OSHA) was established in 1970, which set specific standards for occupational safety and health and began implementing strict laws aimed at protecting workers from occupational hazards.

In Britain, the Health and Safety at Work Act was passed in 1974, which obliges employers to provide a safe working environment and apply specific safety standards. This law significantly improved work environments and reduced the number of occupational accidents.

Occupational Health in the Twenty-first Century

At the beginning of the twenty-first century, the concept of occupational health went beyond physical safety to include mental health and wellness. Organizations recognized the importance of improving workers' mental health and well-being by offering comprehensive wellness programs that include aspects such as stress management, promoting physical activity, and providing psychological support. Many companies and organizations around the world adopted advanced wellness programs that include mental health training, free medical consultations, and healthy nutrition and fitness workshops, reflecting a shift in attention towards achieving a greater work-life balance.

Chapter Three

Challenges
and opportunities
in occupational health
and wellness

With advances in technology, new challenges have emerged in the field of occupational health, including digital stress resulting from the increasing reliance on technology and digital devices, which has led to high levels of stress and fatigue among workers. Companies face challenges in monitoring the health of workers who spend long hours in front of computer screens.

Among the most prominent of these challenges is digital stress and occupational burnout, where workers need psychological support and stress management services, making it necessary to update occupational health strategies to keep rapidly with the changes.

The role of technology in improving occupational health

Technology has significantly advanced occupational health by enabling real time monitoring of workers and predicting potential hazards through the use of smart sensors. Companies use smart devices to monitor the level of stress, heartbeat and other vital indicators that help predict the status of workers.

Modern technologies such as artificial intelligence can also analyze worker data and make recommendations to improve occupational health and reduce risk. For example, AI can identify activities that increase the likelihood of injury in the workplace and suggest appropriate measures to avoid it.

Occupational Health and Wellness During global health crises

The COVID-19 pandemic has significantly impacted occupational health, as it has become necessary to implement new safety standards that include social distancing, wearing masks and disinfecting places regularly. Many companies have committed to remote work and developed new strategies aimed at keeping workers safe.

The COVID-19 pandemic highlighted the importance of occupational health in protecting workers and demonstrated the need for greater resilience in dealing with crises. For example, some companies developed policies that ensure social distancing is maintained inside workplaces, demonstrating the ability of occupational health to adapt to emergency circumstances.

The future of occupational health

As technology continues to advance, occupational health is expected to evolve further, with artificial intelligence and big data enhancing practices and enabling real-time alerts about potential risks. There is also a growing trend towards comprehensive wellness standards that include mental health and work-life balance, making occupational health a vital area for building safe and sustainable work environments.

The history of occupational health is a continuous evolutionary journey that extends from primitive initiatives in ancient times to modern legislation focused on wellness and mental health. This history reflects the importance of achieving safe and sustainable work environments and emphasizes the critical role of occupational health in building prosperous and healthy communities.

Chapter Four

The role of institutions in promoting occupational health and wellness

Organizations play a pivotal role in promoting the occupational health and wellness of workers, not only to achieve compliance with laws and regulations, but also to provide productive and sustainable work environments. Safe work environments reduce accidents and injuries, improve employee performance, and enhance loyalty to the organization, resulting in improved overall productivity. This chapter reviews the role of institutions in promoting occupational health and wellness, with examples and case studies that illustrate the importance of this role and its effective applications.

First: The importance of occupational health and wellness in work environments

Occupational health and wellness are a set of practices and policies aimed at protecting the health and safety of employees, whether related to physical or psychological well-being. Research shows that safe and healthy work environments directly contribute to improved performance and increased job satisfaction.

According to an ILO report, injuries and accidents at work cost around 4% of global GDP annually, highlighting the importance of implementing effective safety policies to reduce these losses. There is growing evidence that organizations that focus on occupational health and wellness achieve remarkable positive results in terms of productivity, reduced absenteeism, and increased job loyalty.

Second: Responsibilities of institutions in providing safe work environments

1. Risk Identification and Assessment:

Organizations have direct responsibility in identifying and assessing risks in the business environment. This requires a comprehensive process that includes analyzing all factors that may affect employee health, whether it's related to equipment, chemicals, or the work environment itself. For example, oil and gas companies assess the risks of exposure to chemicals and the risks associated with heavy machinery as part of their safety strategies.

Case Study: Shell Oil

Shell has launched a program called 'Enhanced Risk Management', where employees at industrial sites are trained to identify and analyze risks on an ongoing basis, and technological systems have been employed to monitor real-time risks. This system has contributed to reducing accidents and reducing downtime resulting from injuries.

2. Application of occupational safety and health standards:

Organizations are committed to applying occupational safety and health standards set by regulators, such as the United States Occupational Safety and Health Administration (OSHA) and ISO standards. This includes using personal protective equipment, providing the necessary training, implementing safety measures such as emergency evacuation plans. Ensuring compliance with these standards is a necessary step to achieve a risk-free work environment.

Global model: Ford Motor Company

Ford has implemented a set of global safety standards that include strict factory work protocols, such as frequent equipment assessments and the design of clear pathways for emergency evacuation of employees. These measures have significantly reduced the rate of injuries, making work environments safer.

3. Continuous training and awareness:

Continuous training on occupational health and safety is essential to help employees understand potential hazards in the work environment and how to deal with them. This also includes training programs on first aid, how to use safety equipment, and awareness of the importance of self-care. Studies have shown that institutions offering periodic training have lower infection rates.

Case Study: Boeing Airlines

Boeing implements intensive safety training programs, where employees are trained to handle heavy equipment and avoid injuries caused by muscle strain. Annual courses are offered that include practical applications and simulation tools for potential incidents. This program has helped reduce injuries and increased employees' awareness of their safety.

4. Promote mental health and wellness:

Besides focusing on physical safety, organizations are beginning to realize the importance of supporting the mental health of employees. These measures can include psychological counseling, employee assistance programs, and policies that support work-life balance. Good mental health improves performance, reduces stress, and increases job satisfaction.

Successful model: Google

Google is known for its well-promoting work environment, with the company offering daily yoga and meditation classes, as well as relaxation rooms and open workspaces that provide a supportive environment. The company also provides confidential psychological counseling service for employees. These initiatives contributed to creating a healthy work culture and increased employee productivity.

5. Continuous Improvement of Safety Practices

Business environments and risks are constantly evolving, necessitating ongoing refinement of safety policies and practices. Organizations must perform regular evaluations of safety protocols and systematically analyze accident and injury data to strengthen preventive measures. Monitoring safety performance is a proven method for enhancing workplace health and safety standards.

Case Study: Nestlé

Nestlé employs a continuous safety enhancement strategy, including monthly assessments of safety metrics and incident reports, comprehensive risk analyses of work environments, and timely policy updates. This proactive approach has led to a notable reduction in workplace injuries and fostered a robust safety culture among employees.

Third: Mechanisms for promoting occupational health and wellness

Strategies to Promote Occupational Health and Wellness

Organizations can adopt the following approaches to prioritize employee health and well-being:

1. Providing internal health services:

Many companies now offer workplace medical clinics and health programs, enabling employees to access immediate care and consultations. These services minimize health-related absenteeism and ensure prompt attention to minor injuries.

Effective Model: ADNOC (UAE)

ADNOC operates on-site medical facilities that provide preventive care services, nutritional guidance, first aid, and health education initiatives. This integrated system has improved employee well-being and significantly reduced absenteeism rates.

2. Wellness and Prevention Programs:

Wellness programs include activities aimed at improving public health such as providing healthy nutrition services, sports initiatives, and stress management workshops. Studies have proven that these programs lead to an increase in the energy and productivity capacity of employees.

Study: Apple's "Fitness First" initiative

Apple offers a "fitness first" program that encourages employees to participate in sports activities and offers free health consultations. The program has contributed to improving the overall health of employees and reducing the incidence of chronic diseases.

3. Design healthy work environments:

Organizations should design healthy work environments that include good lighting, adequate ventilation, and comfortable workspaces. These policies include the design of dedicated relaxation areas that enable employees to recharge during their breaks.

Case Study: Microsoft

Microsoft implements a policy of designing healthy work environments by providing open, naturally lit areas, and offering chairs and stationery designed to avoid muscle strain. This has contributed to improved employee comfort and increased levels of satisfaction.

4. Encourage participation and improve occupational health:

Organizations encourage employees to participate in health and safety promotion, where they are asked for their opinions about work environments and involved in developing improvement plans. This approach has proven that involving employees in improvement processes leads to safer work environments.

Featured Model: FedEx Corporation

FedEx has a policy that allows employees to give feedback and participate in improving safety, offering sessions dedicated to employee suggestions and applying appropriate ones. This policy has contributed to improving safety measures and reducing injuries.

Organizations have a great responsibility in providing safe working environments and promoting occupational health and wellness. By adhering to health policies and practices and rigorously applying safety standards, organizations can enhance productivity and improve the quality of life for employees. It is well established that caring for employees' health and safety not only improves their performance but also enhances the organization's reputation and its ability to attract and retain talent. This underscores the importance of occupational health and wellness in improving performance, health and quality of life.

Medical clinics inside the workplace: A step towards a healthier and more productive work environment

Providing health care within the workplace has become an important trend adopted by many large organizations, recognizing the role of health in boosting productivity and enhancing employee satisfaction. On-site medical clinics and health services offer a practical solution to meet employees' health needs, and deliver multiple benefits, both at the individual and organization levels.

What are the medical clinics inside the workplace?

Medical on-site clinics are specialized health facilities that provide medical and counseling services to employees during working hours. These clinics include a range of services such as:

- Routine medical examinations.
- Providing first aid for minor accidents and injuries.
- General medical consultations.
- Preventive health programs such as awareness of the importance of proper nutrition and physical activity.

The importance of medical clinics in the work environment

1. Quick access to healthcare

On-premises medical clinics provide employees with quick access to medical care without having to leave the workplace. This enables health problems to be addressed at the beginning before they worsen.

2. Reduce absenteeism for health reasons

The presence of nearby health services helps employees receive treatment and health consultations without the need for long sick leaves. This contributes to reducing absenteeism rates and maintains business continuity.

3. Rapid response to accidents and injuries

Medical clinics are equipped to deal with minor accidents and injuries that may occur during work. This reduces the impact of incidents on the workflow and ensures better employee safety.

4. Enhance employee satisfaction

Demonstrating commitment to employee health enhances their sense of appreciation and care by the organization. This, in turn, increases loyalty and job satisfaction, and improves overall productivity and work environment.

Additional benefits for organizations:

1. Boost productivity

When employees are healthy and feel comfortable having medical care nearby, it reflects positively on their level of productivity.

2. Reduce long-term health costs

Medical clinics provide preventive services that reduce the likelihood of employees experiencing serious health problems in the future. This reduces the costs of health insurance and long-term treatment.

3. Improve the reputation of the organization

Organizations that provide internal health services demonstrate a stronger commitment to employee well-being, reinforcing their positive image in the market and helping attract new talent.

Challenges and how to overcome them:

Despite the many benefits, organizations may face challenges in setting up inpatient clinics such as operational costs or providing qualified medical staff. To overcome these challenges, the organization can:

- Collaborate with external health service providers to provide care.
- Establish small clinics providing basic services.
- Invest in preventive programs to reduce future health costs.

Providing medical clinics and health services within the workplace is not just a luxury, it is a smart investment in human capital. These services enhance employee health and satisfaction and ensure a safer and more sustainable work environment.

Organizations that adopt this approach contribute to building a strong and balanced working society, where the health of employees is at the heart of their priorities and concerns.

Facts & Figures:

Caring for employee health is the first step towards achieving excellence and productivity, which makes this initiative one of the best modern practices in human resource management.

Reduce absenteeism from work

According to a study by the American Association for Occupational Health (NSC), companies providing indoor health services saw a 27% reduction in days of absence from work due to health problems compared to companies that did not provide these services.

Improve productivity

According to a study by the Global Wellness Institute, providing health services and preventive programs to employees can increase their productivity by up to 15%, as employees feel comfortable and reassured that medical care is available at work.

Reduce healthcare costs

According to a report by Towers Watson, organizations that offer comprehensive employee health programs have reduced health insurance costs by up to 25% per year. This is due to the reduced need for costly treatments or emergency cases.

Faster response to accidents and injuries

A study from the International Labour Organization (ILO) reported that having on-site medical clinics helped reduce accident response time by 40%, improved employees' chances of recovery and reduced production losses.

Positive impact on employee satisfaction

In a survey conducted by the Global Human Resources Association (SHRM), 89% of employees indicated that access to medical services in the workplace enhances their sense of belonging to the organization, leading to increased loyalty, a better work environment and higher productivity.

Examples from reality

Google Corporation: Offers integrated medical clinics on its premises, which have contributed to a 92% improvement in employee satisfaction, according to an internal assessment.

Apple Corporation: Reports indicate that the presence of inpatient clinics reduced employee absenteeism due to health problems by 30% within the first year of the program's launch.

Investing in prevention

According to a report by the World Health Organization (WHO), every dollar invested in occupational health programs yields a return of $4 through increased productivity and reduced health care costs.

Occupational health programs and their impact on public health and productivity

Occupational health programs are a key component of organizational strategies aimed at supporting employee health and safety and enhancing overall well-being, thereby improving organizational performance. These programs seek to promote public health, reduce workplace injuries, and provide both medical and psychological support, contributing to the creation of positive work environments. In this chapter, we will explore the concept of occupational health programs, their significance, and their positive impact on public health and productivity, supported by practical models and studies that demonstrate their effect on institutional performance.

First: The concept of occupational health programs

Occupational health programs are a set of policies and practices designed to support the physical and psychological well-being of employees. These programs cover various aspects, including disease prevention, primary health care services, mental health promotion, and training employees in safe health practices. The ultimate goal is to create a health-friendly work environment where employees feel valued and cared for by their organization.

Second: The importance of occupational health programs

1. Prevention of diseases and injuries:

Occupational health programs aim to prevent work-related diseases and injuries resulting from hazardous work environments. Employees are provided with training on ways to prevent common work-related illnesses, such as muscle strain, injuries caused by heavy lifting, and exposure to dangerous chemicals.

2. Promote mental health and wellness:

Mental health has become an integral part of occupational health programs, as studies show that chronic stress negatively affects productivity and quality of life. Therefore, some institutions provide psychological counseling and support to employees with the aim of managing stress and improving mental health.

3. Increase job loyalty and reduce absenteeism:

An organization's concern for employee health is a motivating factor for loyalty and job commitment, as employees feel valued and important to their organization. Studies have shown that the implementation of effective occupational health programs contributes to reducing absenteeism rates and increasing employee satisfaction with work.

4. Achieving sustainability and social responsibility goals:

Occupational health programs align sustainability and corporate social responsibility goals, reflecting an organization's commitment to the well-being of its employees and broader society. This, in turn, enhances the organization's reputation and increases its appeal to both customers and investors.

Third: The impact of occupational health programs on public health and productivity

Research and studies have shown that occupational health programs have a significant impact on overall health and productivity. Several studies have provided models that illustrate the positive impact of these programs, including:

1. Improve overall health and reduce medical costs:

Occupational health programs are an effective way to improve the overall health of employees and reduce medical costs for the organization. A Harvard study showed that companies that invest in occupational health programs make savings of up to $3 per dollar spent on health care due to reducing chronic diseases and improving overall health.

Case Study: Johnson & Johnson

Johnson & Johnson is a pioneer in providing occupational health programs, offering comprehensive programs that include regular medical check-ups, health consultations, and various wellness programs. These programs have reduced the incidence of chronic diseases among employees by 34% and achieved significant savings in healthcare costs.

2. Improve productivity and reduce absenteeism:

Improving the overall health of employees reduces the number of sick days, thereby contributing to increased productivity. A study by Rand Corporation showed that companies implementing occupational health programs reduce absence days by about 25% and improve productivity levels.

Case Study: The Coca-Cola Company

Coca-Cola offers comprehensive occupational health programs, including health education campaigns on nutrition, physical activity initiatives, and stress management training. These programs have resulted in reduced absenteeism and a 20% increase in productivity.

3. Reduce stress and improve psychological performance

Occupational health programs contribute to creating psychologically supportive work environments by offering mental health support and counseling services that help employees manage daily stressors. A study by the World Health Organization (WHO) shows that organizations that provide mental health support programs experience increased employee satisfaction and a 40% reduction in stress levels.

Featured Model: Microsoft Corporation

Microsoft offers mental health programs that include counseling sessions and stress management training, which have helped improve employees' mental well-being and reduce stress levels. These initiatives have enhanced employee performance and increased productivity.

4. Boost morale and motivate employees

Studies show that providing occupational health and wellness programs raises employee morale and increases motivation. When employees feel that their organization values their health and well-being, they are more engaged and willing to perform at their best.

Case Study: Google

Google offers a variety of occupational health support programs, including relaxation spaces, yoga classes, fitness activities, and mental health support. These programs have significantly boosted employee morale and motivation, resulting in higher job satisfaction and improved productivity.

Fourth: Challenges Facing Occupational Health Programs

Despite the clear benefits of occupational health programs, organizations may face several challenges in implementing them effectively, including:

- **Financial costs:**

Establishing effective health programs often requires significant investment in infrastructure, services, and specialized personnel, which may be a barrier for some institutions, especially smaller ones.

- **Employee engagement:**

Some employees may lack motivation or interest in participating in wellness programs. This makes it essential for organizations to develop engaging strategies and foster a culture that encourages participation and commitment.

- **Monitoring and evaluation:**

To ensure long term success, organizations must implement systems to regularly assess the effectiveness of health programs. This includes analyzing data related to employee health and productivity to guide continuous improvement.

Fifth: Strategies for implementing effective health programs

To achieve the benefits of occupational health programs, organizations must adopt strategies that ensure successful implementation and sustainability, including:

1. Building health supportive culture:

Effective health programs begin with cultivating a workplace culture that values and supports employee well-being. This includes active support from senior leadership and the presence of positive role models who promote healthy behaviors and lead by example.

2. Providing comprehensive, inclusive services:

Occupational health programs should address a broad spectrum of needs, from physical and mental health to nutrition and preventive care. Offering a variety of services ensures that the diverse need of employees is met, which in turn increases participation and program impact.

3. Encouraging participation and motivation:

Organizations can boost engagement by offering incentives for participation, such as rewards for meeting health goals. Hosting wellness challenges, fitness competitions, or health -themed events can also foster a sense of community and make well initiatives more enjoyable.

4. Continuous evaluation and development:

Organizations should periodically monitor and evaluate the effectiveness of occupational health programs. Ongoing assessment helps identify areas for improvement and ensure that programs evolve in response to the changing needs of employees.

Occupational health programs are a strategic investment that enable organizations to achieve both their productive and social responsibility goals. By supporting employee well-being, reducing absenteeism and boosting performance, these programs contribute to creating a healthy and stimulating work environment.

Implementing occupational health and wellness programs reflects an organization's genuine commitment to its people and recognition of their value. This not only benefits employees but also strengthens the organization as a whole, enhancing its competitiveness and long-term success in the marketplace.

Improving performance and reducing occupational accidents

Improving performance and reducing occupational accidents are strategic priorities for organizations aiming to foster productive and sustainable work environments. Occupational health and safety policies and programs play a critical role in achieving these goals. A safe and supportive workplace not only enhances employee productivity but also reduces the costs associated with accidents and injuries.

Achieving these goals requires the implementation of comprehensive strategies that promote both individual performance and a strong culture of safety. In this chapter, we will explore effective methods for enhancing performance, emphasize the importance of minimizing occupational incidents, and present case studies and research findings that demonstrate the organizational benefits of adopting these practices.

First: The importance of improving performance in the work environment

Performance improvement is a continuous process aimed at increasing employee efficiency and effectiveness, enabling organizations to achieve their goals more quickly and professionally. By adopting performance-focused procedures and policies, organizations can enhance the quality of their services or products, strengthen their competitiveness, and create safer and more engaging work environments.

Several studies have shown that improving workplace performance not only boosts productivity but also supports employees' mental well-being. When employees feel recognized and valued, their job satisfaction rises, leading to greater motivation and long-term commitment.

Second: The importance of reducing occupational accidents

Occupational accidents impose a significant burden on organizations in terms of financial costs and in lost time due to employee injuries. Beyond the tangible losses, accidents can lower employee morale and damage an organization's reputation. Therefore, minimizing workplace accidents is important for reducing losses and protecting the health and safety of the workforce.

According to a report by the International Labour Organization (ILO), occupational accidents and injuries cost the global economy approximately 4% of GDP annually. This figure highlights the importance of prevention and the implementation of performance improvement programs to reduce these impacts.

Third: Strategies to improve performance and reduce occupational accidents

To effectively enhance performance and reduce occupational accidents, organizations must adopt strategies that increase employee awareness and ensure safe working environments.

Below are some strategies that have proven effective in this area:

1. Continuous Occupational Safety Training:

Continuous safety training is one of the most important tools to improve performance and reduce occupational accidents. Through regular sessions, employees gain essential knowledge about safe work practices, proper equipment use, preventive measures, and emergency procedures. Research shows that organizations providing consistent safety training experience significantly lower rates of workplace accidents.

Effective model: Boeing Airlines

Boeing is a company that implements comprehensive safety training programs, where employees are periodically trained to handle heavy equipment and manage potential hazards. This program has resulted in a 30% reduction in accident rates and increased employee awareness of safety.

2. Developing a culture of safety in the work environment:

Building an organizational culture that encourages safety and prioritizes it is one of the most important ways to help reduce occupational accidents. This requires support from senior management and an emphasis on the importance of safety in all aspects of daily operations.

Employees should feel that safety is not just a policy, but a core organizational value.

Case Study: Dunham Shipping Company

Dunham has developed a comprehensive safety culture aimed at enabling employees to participate in improving safety procedures. This approach has significantly reduced accidents and created a work environment where employees feel responsible for their safety and that of their colleagues.

3. Applying modern technology for safety monitoring:

Technology has become one of the modern tools that help improve performance and provide safe working environments. Systems are used to continuously monitor hazards, such as thermal cameras, early warning systems, and sensors that monitor the status of equipment. These tools help in early detection and risk management before accidents occur.

Effective model: Shell Oil

Shell has employed technological monitoring systems that help identify immediate hazards, such as gas leaks or rising temperatures. The use of this technology has reduced accidents and enhanced workplace safety across all the company's sites.

4. Conducting periodic evaluation and analysis of accident data:

Continuous assessment of incidents and analysis of their causes helps organizations identify vulnerabilities and take preventive action. Moreover, organizations can analyze incident data to identify recurring patterns and common causes, helping them develop effective plans to minimize future incidents.

Case Study: Nestlé

Nestlé conducts regular safety assessments that include a comprehensive analysis of each incident recorded within the work environment, where causes are analyzed and strategies for their prevention are developed. This approach has reduced the accident rate by 25% over five years.

5. **Encouraging open communication and risk communication:**

Encouraging employees to report risks and vulnerabilities in the work environment without fear of penalties enhances the culture of safety and contributes to reducing accidents. Employees play a key role in the early detection of potential hazards, enabling the organization to take corrective action quickly.

Effective Model: The Coca-Cola Company

Coca-Cola implements an open communication policy that allows employees to report any risks they may face. This policy fosters a reporting culture without fear of penalties, which has enhanced employees' awareness of identifying risks before they escalate into actual incidents.

Fourth: The Impact of Improving Performance and Reducing Accidents on Institutional Performance

1. **Increased Productivity and Improved Overall Performance**

By reducing incidents and enhancing the work environment, employees can perform their tasks more efficiently. A safe work environment boosts employees' focus and psychological well-being, which positively reflects productivity.

Case Study: The Impact of Safety on Productivity at Ford Motor Company

A study conducted by Ford Motor Company indicated that reducing incidents led to a 15% increase in productivity, as the safe work environment contributed to enhancing performance levels and reducing unexpected downtime.

2. Reducing Costs Associated with Accidents and Injuries

Organizations incur high costs due to accidents, whether in the form of compensation, healthcare expenses, or production losses. Reducing accidents leads to lowering these costs and achieving significant economic savings.

Effective Model: Toyota

Toyota implements a zero-accident policy, focusing on minimizing risks in all aspects of operations. This has resulted in reduced costs related to compensation and injuries, contributing to improved company budgeting and increased profits.

3. Enhancing Employee Morale and Increasing Satisfaction:

A safe work environment makes employees feel that their safety and well-being matter to the organization, boosting their morale and increasing job satisfaction. Studies show that employee satisfaction rises when they feel secure in the workplace, reducing turnover and absenteeism rates.

Case Study: Johnson & Johnson

Johnson & Johnson implemented advanced safety programs that positively impacted employee satisfaction. Company data indicated a significant increase in employee satisfaction and improved morale due to efforts to ensure a safe work environment.

Improving performance and reducing occupational incidents are fundamental pillars that provide organizations with numerous economic and moral benefits. By adopting well-planned strategies and innovative techniques, organizations can create safe work environments that enhance productivity efficiency and minimize accidents. Employees in safe workplaces contribute more effectively to achieving organizational goals and feel part of an institutional culture that respects and supports their well-being

Continuous Evaluation of Accidents and Analysis of Their Causes: A Proactive Approach to Prevention and Safety Improvement

Workplace accidents remain a major challenge for organizations across all sectors, as they can lead to significant human and economic losses. To address these challenges, the continuous evaluation of accidents and analysis of their causes serve as effective tools to help organizations identify weaknesses in their systems and implement preventive measures to reduce the likelihood of recurrence.

Importance of Continuous Accident Evaluation

1. Improving the Work Environment
Analyzing accident data helps uncover hidden risks, leading to a safer and more secure work environment.

2. Reducing Economic Costs
According to a study by the International Labour Organization (ILO), occupational accidents cost the global economy approximately 3.94% of GDP annually. Continuous evaluation helps mitigate these costs through prevention.

3. Increasing Employee Productivity
A safe work environment boosts employee confidence and motivates them to work more efficiently.

Analyzing Accident Causes and Their Role in Prevention

1. Identifying Recurring Patterns

Accident analysis enables organizations to recognize recurring patterns, such as:

- Work locations where accidents frequently occur.
- Times or conditions with heightened risks.

Example: A study by the U.S. Occupational Safety and Health Administration (OSHA) revealed that 60% of industrial accidents result from negligence in equipment maintenance.

2. Understanding Root Causes

In-depth analysis helps pinpoint root causes, which may include:

- Inadequate employee training.
- Lack of preventive equipment or procedures.
- Employee fatigue due to workload pressure.

3. Developing Effective Preventive Plans

Based on analysis, organizations can:

- Design targeted employee training programs.
- Enhance safety standards and provide modern equipment.
- Implement flexible work schedules to reduce employee fatigue.

By adopting these strategies, organizations can foster safer workplaces, minimize risks, and achieve long-term operational and financial benefits.

Supporting Figures and Statistics

Reduction in Accident Rates:

According to a report by the National Safety Council (NSC), organizations that rely on accident analysis and implement preventive plans have reduced accident rates by 30% to 40% over five years.

Positive Financial Impact:

A study by the World Health Organization (WHO) found that every dollar invested in improving occupational safety saves $4 in costs related to injuries and absenteeism.

Root Causes:

A study by OSHA revealed that 76% of accidents resulted from preventable causes, such as lack of training or unsafe equipment.

Steps to Implement Continuous Evaluation and Accident Analysis

1. Collect Data Accurately

- Record all accidents, regardless of severity.
- Use advanced electronic tools to store and analyze data.

2. Analyze Data

- Identify recurring patterns using data analysis techniques.
- Conduct employee interviews to understand the circumstances of each incident.

3. Develop Preventive Plans

- Design training programs based on analysis results.
- Improve preventive procedures and equipment.

4. Continuous Review

- Conduct periodic evaluations of the effectiveness of preventive plans.

- Adjust plans based on new developments or changes in the work environment.

Impact of Continuous Evaluation on Organizations

- **Enhancing Organizational Reputation:**

Organizations that prioritize occupational safety and demonstrate tangible efforts to reduce accidents gain a positive market reputation.

- **Increasing Employee Loyalty:**

A safe work environment boosts employee loyalty and encourages long-term retention.

- **Achieving Regulatory Compliance:**

Commitment to accident analysis and preventive planning helps organizations comply with local and international safety standards.

- Continuous evaluation of accidents and analysis of their causes is not just a precautionary measure-it is a strategic investment that saves lives, reduces costs, and enhances productivity. Organizations adopting this approach contribute to building a safe and sustainable work environment, benefiting employees and society as a whole.

- In conclusion, while accidents may be inevitable, preparedness and learning from them are what distinguish between successful organizations.

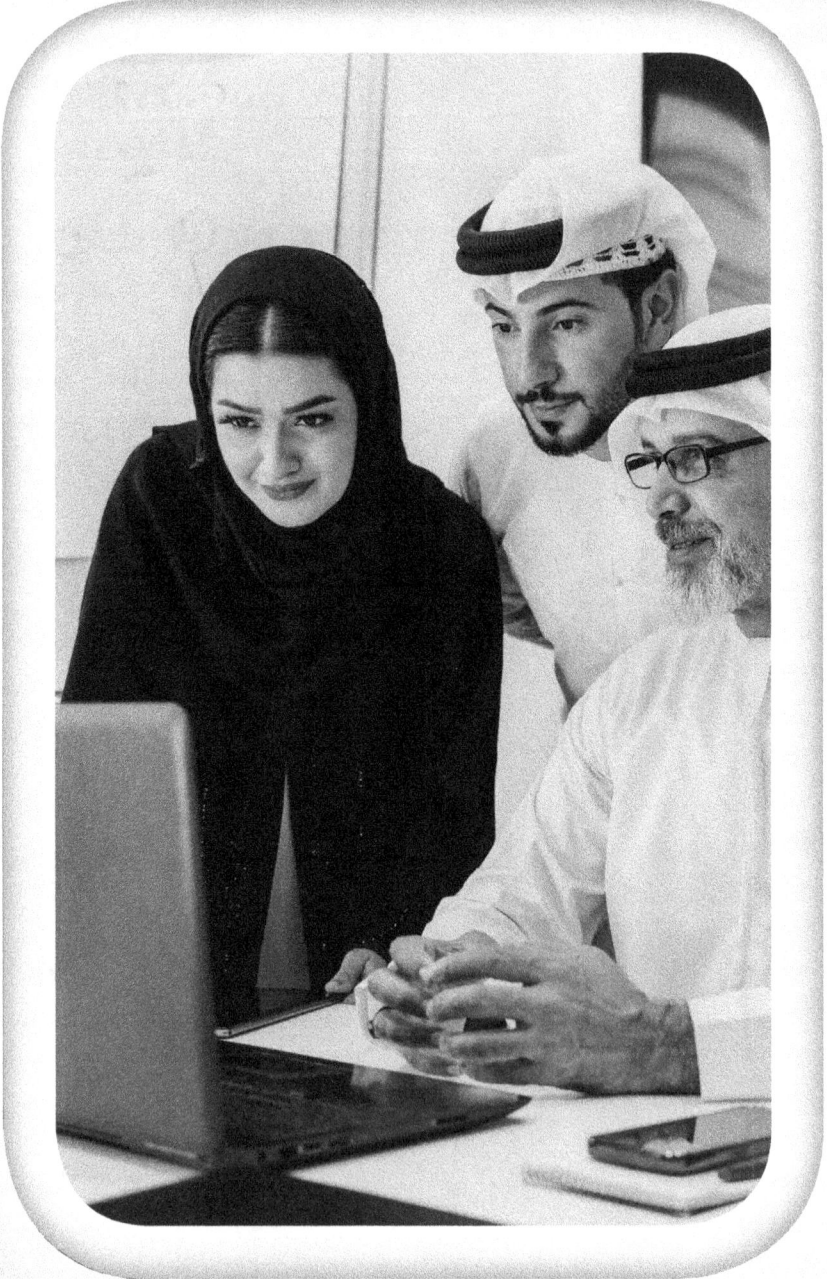

Chapter Five

Enhancing Occupational Health and Wellness in the UAE

Occupational health and wellness play a pivotal role in achieving sustainable development, improving productivity, and enhancing quality of life in the United Arab Emirates. In recent years, the UAE has demonstrated significant commitment to promoting healthy and safe work environments, developing legislation and standards that ensure the safety and well-being of workers across all sectors. This chapter reviews the current state of occupational health and wellness in the UAE, highlighting the legislation and initiatives implemented to ensure healthy, sustainable, and secure work environments.

First: Current State of Occupational Health and Wellness in the UAE

The UAE is among the nations experiencing rapid economic growth and remarkable development across various fields, leading to an increasing need to improve work environments and enhance occupational health and safety. The country strives to safeguard the health and safety of all workers, whether in the public or private sector, by applying the highest global standards. The current state of occupational health and wellness in the UAE can be summarized as follows:

1. Increased Awareness of Occupational Health and Wellness Importance

Institutions in the UAE have recognized that employee health and safety are fundamental components of their strategies. Prioritizing occupational health and wellness boosts employee morale, increases productivity, and reduces absenteeism rates.

2. Growing Focus on Work-Life Balance

The UAE's labor sector is witnessing a notable shift toward

providing work environments that enable employees to achieve a balance between their personal and professional lives. This balance is integral to occupational health and wellness, positively impacting employee satisfaction and performance.

3. **Expansion of Occupational Health, Wellness, and Awareness Programs**

Many UAE-based organizations implement comprehensive occupational health and wellness programs, including sports activities, medical services, and awareness campaigns aimed at improving employees' lifestyles and enhancing public health.

4. **Adoption of Technology to Monitor and Improve Occupational Health**

The UAE widely embraces technology in occupational health. Many companies rely on innovations such as smart devices to measure employee health, monitor work environments, and implement early warning systems for accidents.

Second: Legislation Related to Occupational Health and Wellness in the UAE

The UAE has established stringent legislation and laws to ensure the safety and health of workers across all sectors. These regulations include directives to protect workers from hazards, enhance safety, and provide healthy work environments. Below are the most prominent of these legislations:

1. **Federal Labor Law (Federal Law No. 33 of 2021):**

The Federal Labor Law serves as the legal framework regulating workers' rights and obligations. It includes provisions outlining employers' duties toward employee safety and health, such as the requirement to provide protective equipment and ensure a safe and healthy working environment.

2. **Decisions by the Ministry of Human Resources and Emiratization (2022):**

The Ministry of Human Resources and Emiratization has issued several decisions and regulations aimed at promoting occupational health and safety. Notable among these are mandates requiring organizations to implement safety measures to reduce workplace accidents and injuries. These regulations include specific guidelines for safety in construction sites, handling chemical substances, and operating heavy machinery.

3. **Occupational Hazards Protection Law (Federal Law No. 33 of 2021):**

This law aims to protect workers from risks arising from their job nature, such as exposure to harmful substances, hazards in confined spaces, or working with electrical equipment. It outlines safety standards that organizations must follow to mitigate these risks.

4. **Environmental and Health Legislation:**

The UAE adopts strict environmental laws to ensure workplaces are healthy and free from public health hazards. Companies are required to comply with environmental standards set by relevant authorities to maintain safe and healthy work environments for employees and the community.

5. **Abu Dhabi Occupational Safety and Health Initiative (2006) (OSHAD):**

This initiative, launched by the Abu Dhabi government, aims to elevate occupational safety and health standards in the emirate. In

2010, the Abu Dhabi Occupational Safety and Health Centre (OSHAD) was established. OSHAD sets safety standards and guidelines for all sectors, obliging companies to implement occupational health programs and submit periodic safety reports.

6. Role of the Abu Dhabi Department of Health (DoH) and Dubai Health Authority (DHA):

The Abu Dhabi Department of Health and Dubai Health Authority play a pivotal role in advancing occupational health by setting health standards and regulations. These entities enforce monitoring systems to ensure corporate compliance with laws and provide necessary guidance and support.

Third: National Initiatives to Promote Occupational Health and Wellbeing

The UAE seeks to improve the occupational health and wellness of workers through a number of national initiatives aimed at raising awareness and implementing better health and safety practices, the most prominent of which are:

1. "National Program for Happiness and Positivity" Initiative:

This initiative aims to create positive work environments and enhance employee well-being. The program encourages organizations to adopt health policies that support work-life balance and help employees improve their mental and physical health.

2. "Emirates Without Smoking" campaign:

This campaign aims to combat smoking and promote awareness of its harms, as it encourages organizations to implement smoke-free policies and provide healthy work environments for employees, and the campaign includes awareness programs and initiatives that help employees quit smoking.

3. "Fitness" Initiative:

Many companies in the UAE have adopted fitness promotion programs, which aim to promote healthy habits among employees. These programs include signing up for sports clubs and offering sports classes such as yoga and others within the work environment, which helps improve fitness and overall health.

4. Mental health initiatives in the workplace:

The UAE offers mental health programs aimed at enhancing the psychological well-being of employees, such as psychological counseling programs and support services that help employees cope with psychological stress. These initiatives seek to improve mental health, which reflects positively on overall performance in the workplace.

The importance of promoting physical fitness within work:
Benefits and supportive studies

With increasing working hours and less physical activity in daily life, promoting fitness within work environments has become vital. The integration of fitness programs is not just a luxury, it is an investment in the health and productivity of employees, which reflects positively on the performance of organizations and the well-being of society as a whole.

Benefits of Fitness Enhancement at Work

1. Improve the overall health of employees

Regular physical activity reduces the risk of chronic diseases such as heart disease, diabetes, and high blood pressure. According to the World Health Organization (WHO), physical activity can reduce the risk of chronic diseases by 25%.

2. Increase productivity

Studies conducted by the University of Leeds Beckett showed that employees who engage in physical activity during working hours showed a 15% increase in their productivity compared to others.

3. Improve the psychological state

Exercise contributes to reducing levels of anxiety and depression and promoting feelings of satisfaction. A report by the American Psychiatric Association (APA) confirmed that 30 minutes of exercise a day reduces anxiety symptoms by 30%.

4. Reduce absenteeism from work

Fitness programs help reduce absenteeism due to diseases associated with lack of movement. A report from Rand Europe showed that companies implementing fitness programs saw a 23% reduction in employee absences.

5. Promote social interaction and morale

Group sports activities within the work strengthen relationships between employees, which improves the work environment and increases positive interaction.

Supporting figures and studies
Return on investment in occupational health and fitness

According to a study by Towers Watson, every dollar invested in fitness programs yields a return of up to $6 by reducing health care costs and increasing productivity.

Impact on public health

A report from the Harvard School of Public Health showed that employees who participate in regular sports activities enjoy a 32% reduction in chronic disease rates.

Improve cognitive performance

Research conducted by Stanford University shows that walking for 10 minutes during working hours improves cognitive performance by 20%, promoting creative thinking and problem solving.

Reduce work-related injuries

A fitness program implemented at a major manufacturer in the United States has reduced work-related injuries by 50% in just two years.

How to implement fitness programs at work

1. Allocate dedicated sports spaces

Establishing small gyms or open areas for sports inside the workplace.

Provide sports equipment such as treadmills or stationary bicycles.

2. Organize group activities

Organize group exercise sessions such as yoga or aerobic exercise.

Holding sports competitions between departments to promote team spirit

3. Incorporate physical activity into the daily routine

Encourage meetings while walking rather than sitting.

Provide short breaks for stretching or light sports.

4. Provide incentives

Provide rewards to employees who achieve certain fitness goals.

Sign up for local sports clubs as part of employee benefits.

5. Awareness and education

Organizing awareness workshops on the importance of fitness.

Distributing educational materials on the health benefits of physical activity.

Successful models

Google:

The company offers a range of sports activities within its offices, including yoga sessions and personal fitness programs, resulting in 91% employee satisfaction.

Microsoft:

Athletic programs with fitness challenges are implemented between departments, increasing employee engagement and reducing absenteeism rates by 22%.

Enhancing fitness within work is not just an additional option, it is a necessity to improve employee health, increase productivity and enhance the work environment. By implementing comprehensive athletic programs, organizations can achieve significant benefits including improved performance, reduced health costs, and building a positive and sustainable work culture.

Ultimately, investing in fitness is an investment in human capital, which puts organizations on the path to sustainable success.

Fourth: The Impact of Legislation and Initiatives on the Work Environment in the UAE

The legislation and initiatives implemented by the UAE have significantly impacted on the work environment and employee safety, fostering a strong culture of occupational health and safety across various sectors. Key outcomes of these efforts include:

1. Increased Awareness of Occupational Health and Safety:

Government efforts have raised awareness among organizations and employees about the importance of occupational health and safety, reducing accident rates and improving workplace performance.

2. Improved Quality of Life for Employees:

National initiatives and stringent legislation enhance employees' quality of life by ensuring higher levels of workplace safety, boosting morale, and increasing loyalty to organizations.

3. Reduced Costs Associated with Accidents and Injuries:

Thanks to health-focused legislation and initiatives, many UAE companies have reduced costs linked to occupational accidents and injury-related compensation. This strengthens organizations' financial sustainability and enables greater investment in improving work environments.

4. Enhanced Productivity and Efficiency:

Healthy and sustainable work environments are key to improving productivity. Supporting employee health and safety allows them to work with greater focus and efficiency, effectively contributing to organizational goals.

5. Strengthened Corporate Reputation:

Companies that adopt occupational health and safety policies enhance their reputation and appeal to customers and investors. Organizations committed to health and safety standards are viewed as credible and trustworthy.

The UAE has made significant progress in promoting occupational health and well-being through continuous efforts, advanced legislation, and national initiatives that support safe and healthy work environments. These policies reflect the nation's commitment to employee health and safety, emphasizing that healthy workplaces are not a luxury but a cornerstone of sustainable development and economic growth. Improving occupational health and well-being is fundamental to achieving productive and sustainable work environments in the UAE, serving as a model for the region and the world.

ADNOC: A Pioneering Model in Occupational Health

Abu Dhabi National Oil Company (ADNOC) stands as a leading example in occupational health. Its operations are rooted in a commitment to the highest standards of health and safety, not only to protect its employees but also to promote safe and sustainable work environments in the energy sector. ADNOC's approach to occupational health revolves around safeguarding its employees, contractors, and the communities it operates in, reflecting a holistic vision for safe and healthy workplaces that drive sustainable growth and high productivity.

First: ADNOC's Commitment to Occupational Health and Safety

Safety is an integral part of ADNOC's culture, as the company's daily operations reflect a strategic direction that prioritizes the health and safety of its workforce. Through its policies and procedures, ADNOC aims to ensure all employees return home safely at the end of each day. The company embraces a philosophy that worker safety directly enhances performance and ensures long-term productivity sustainability.

1. Safety-First Culture:

ADNOC recognizes that creating a healthy and safe work

environment heavily relies on instilling a safety-first culture within the organization, starting from senior leadership and permeating all organizational levels. The company believes safety is not merely a regulatory requirement but a core value that builds trust with employees and stakeholders.

2. Continuous Training and Safety Awareness:

ADNOC is committed to providing comprehensive training programs for its employees to enhance their awareness of safe practices and empower them to identify and efficiently address potential risks. These programs include training sessions on risk management, emergency response procedures, and the use of personal protective equipment (PPE).

Second: ADNOC's Occupational Health Framework

ADNOC's occupational health framework consists of a set of innovative policies and practices aimed at continuously monitoring and improving working conditions. The company is committed to providing risk-free work environments and implements an integrated occupational health and safety system based on risk assessment and ensuring compliance with preventive measures.

1. Risk Management and Control:

ADNOC has identified a comprehensive list of potential risks in work environments and developed strategies to manage these risks effectively. A thorough risk assessment is conducted across multiple stages, from exploration operations to production and transportation. These assessments are regularly updated to ensure the ongoing effectiveness of preventive measures.

2. Emergency Planning:

ADNOC adopts immediate emergency response procedures, including specific guidelines for accidents that may occur during operations. This approach is part of the company's strategy to safeguard employees and protect them from potential harm. These procedures encompass evacuation plans, first-aid training, and emergency response tools that enable employees to handle crises promptly.

3. Technology in Safety Monitoring:

ADNOC utilizes advanced technology to monitor safety at work sites. These technologies include thermal cameras, early warning systems, and sensors to monitor equipment conditions and detect risks proactively. These systems allow the company to address immediate risks and reduce accidents efficiently.

Third: ADNOC's Ten Personal Safety Rules

ADNOC has established ten personal safety rules to prevent accidents and injuries and ensure a safe and suitable work environment for all employees. These rules represent a set of fundamental procedures that must be followed across various operations, aligned with the best global practices. The rules include:

1. Work with a valid permit when required: Ensure obtaining necessary work permits, especially in high-safety-risk areas.

2. Obtain a permit before entering confined spaces: To guarantee employee safety when working in enclosed spaces with heightened risks.

3. Ensure electrical sources are isolated: To prevent electrical accidents and related injuries.

4. Obtain prior authorization before disabling or bypassing safety controls: This ensures full compliance with safety protocols.

5. Protection from falls in elevated areas: Includes using fall protection equipment when working at heights.

6. Plan lifting operations and secure the surrounding area: To ensure safe lifting processes when handling heavy equipment.

7. Follow safety rules when handling toxic gases: To minimize health risks associated with exposure to such gases.

8. Adhere to safe driving procedures: Includes complying with traffic rules and safe driving practices within and outside work sites.

9. Protect oneself and others from fire hazards: Involves using firefighting equipment and avoiding improper handling of flammable materials.

10. Control flammable materials: Includes implementing strict measures to prevent fire-related incidents.

Fourth: ADNOC's Occupational Health Initiatives

ADNOC relies on diverse initiatives to enhance occupational health and create a safe work environment for its employees. These initiatives are part of the company's strategy to reduce accidents and improve overall safety in workplaces. Among these initiatives are:

1. ADNOC Safety Day:

Safety Day is an annual event aimed at raising awareness about the importance of occupational health and safety among employees and contractors. The day includes awareness activities, lectures, and workshops that encourage employees to adopt safety practices as an integral part of their daily lives.

2. "Overcome the Heat" Campaign:

Given the UAE's hot climate, ADNOC launched the "Overcome the Heat" campaign to educate employees about the importance of protecting themselves from heat stress while working outdoors. The campaign provides guidelines on drinking sufficient water, wearing appropriate clothing, and taking regular rest breaks.

3. "I Make a Difference" Campaign:

This campaign encourages employees to take responsibility for their personal safety and the safety of their colleagues. It urges them to commit to implementing the Ten Safety Rules and to actively participate in improving safety practices in the workplace.

4. Mental Health Initiatives:

ADNOC recognizes the importance of mental health and offers psychological support and counselling programs to help employees address psychological challenges they may face in the work environment.

Fifth: International Recognition and Achievements in Occupational Safety

ADNOC has earned numerous international certifications and accreditations that reflect its commitment to global occupational health and safety standards, such as the ISO 45001 certification, which reinforces the company's position as a leader in occupational health. ADNOC's attainment of these certifications represents international recognition of its efforts to create safe and healthy work environments and underscores its commitment to continuous innovation in safety practices.

Sixth: The Impact of ADNOC's Role in Occupational Health on the Work Environment

ADNOC's efforts in occupational health have contributed to creating a safe and thriving work environment. The impact of its role can be summarized as follows:

1. Increased Productivity and Reduced Accidents:

Thanks to its safety programs and awareness initiatives, ADNOC has established safer work environments, leading to fewer accidents and higher productivity. Employees feel secure and comfortable while working, enhancing their ability to focus and innovate.

2. Enhanced Employee Loyalty and Morale:

ADNOC's focus on employee safety and well-being has strengthened staff loyalty, as employees recognize the company's prioritization of their protection and welfare.

3. Lower Accident-Related Costs:

By reducing accidents, ADNOC has successfully decreased costs associated with workplace injuries and worker compensation, achieving significant savings that bolster the company's sustainability.

4. Improved International Reputation:

ADNOC has received international acclaim for its occupational health initiatives, solidifying its reputation as a leader in providing safe and healthy workplaces. This recognition positions ADNOC as a benchmark in the energy sector.

ADNOC represents a pioneering model in advancing occupational health and safety, reaffirming its unwavering commitment to developing innovative and sustainable health policies and practices. The company fosters a work environment rooted in employee safety, preventive culture, and safety awareness. ADNOC's role in occupational health is not merely a regulatory obligation but part of its mission to achieve a safe and sustainable future in the energy industry. This makes ADNOC an exemplary entity in the UAE, the region, and the world.

Occupational Health Challenges in the UAE
Development Opportunities

The United Arab Emirates faces diverse challenges in occupational health due to its harsh climate and the vast cultural diversity of its workforce. These challenges require specialized strategies and programs focused on meeting employees' needs and ensuring their safety and well-being in an advanced and diverse work environment. Despite these challenges, these conditions present significant opportunities for innovation and development in occupational health programs.

In this chapter, we will explore the occupational health challenges in the UAE, strategies to address them, and development opportunities that can elevate workplace safety and efficiency to new levels.

First: Climatic Challenges and Their Impact on Occupational Health

The UAE's harsh climate is characterized by extremely high summer temperatures, sometimes exceeding 50°C, high humidity, and prolonged exposure to direct sunlight. These conditions significantly affect occupational health, particularly for outdoor workers or those in physically demanding roles. To mitigate risks, a mandatory midday work ban has been enforced, prohibiting outdoor work between 12:30 PM and 3:00 PM from June 15 to September 15 annually. This policy aims to protect workers from heat-related hazards during peak temperatures.

Exemptions from the Midday Work Ban

The following tasks are exempt for technical or emergency reasons:

1. Asphalt laying and concrete pouring if they cannot be paused or completed after the ban period.
2. Emergency repairs to prevent public hazards (e.g., water pipeline failures).
3. Work requiring government permits due to impacts on traffic flow or public safety.

For details, refer to Article 3 of Ministerial Decision No. 44 of 2022 and the midday work ban clause in Administrative Decision No. 19 of 2023 on Occupational Health and Safety Procedures.

1. Heat Stress and Heatstroke

Outdoor workers, such as those in construction, oil and gas, or physically intensive roles, are at risk of heat stress or heatstroke due to high temperatures and humidity. Without preventive measures, this can lead to dehydration, dizziness, loss of consciousness, or even death.

2. Ventilation and Air Conditioning Challenges

Indoor workplaces must maintain effective air conditioning and ventilation systems to ensure air quality and comfortable temperatures, especially given extreme external heat.

3. Sudden Weather Changes and Safety Risks

Sandstorms and abrupt weather shifts in the UAE can reduce visibility and impair breathing, increasing accident risks for outdoor workers.

Strategies to Address Climatic Challenges

1. Implementing the "Overcome the Heat" Program

This initiative educates workers on heat management, including:

- Drinking sufficient water.
- Wearing lightweight, breathable clothing.
- Scheduling work during cooler morning or evening hours.

2. Enhancing Ventilation and Air Conditioning Systems

Advanced climate control systems are critical to maintaining healthy indoor temperatures and minimizing the impact of external heat.

3. Continuous Training for Extreme Weather Conditions

Companies provide training on handling sandstorms or extreme heat, such as using face masks for dust protection or halting work during dangerously low visibility.

Key Takeaway:

The UAE's occupational health challenges demand proactive measures, but they also drive innovation in safety practices. By prioritizing worker well-being through policies like the midday ban and targeted programs, the UAE continues to set benchmarks for occupational health in harsh climates.)

Second: Cultural Diversity and Its Impact on Occupational Health

The UAE's workforce is distinguished by its remarkable cultural diversity, with employees from various nationalities and cultural backgrounds. While this diversity enriches the workplace, it poses unique challenges for occupational health, as employees' needs and perceptions of health and safety practices often vary.

1. Disparities in Understanding and Acceptance of Safety Practices

Employees' understanding of safety rules varies based on their cultural and educational backgrounds, leading to differences in compliance with health and safety protocols. Some nationalities may be unfamiliar with high safety standards, necessitating additional awareness efforts to ensure proper implementation of safety practices.

2. Language Barriers and Communication Challenges

The multilingual nature of the workforce complicates the communication of health and safety information. Linguistically diverse workplaces require guidelines and instructions to be provided in multiple languages to ensure effective dissemination of critical information to all employees.

3. Dietary Habits and Their Impact on Nutrition and Public Health

Cultural diversity influences dietary preferences, which can affect employees' overall health. Some workers may lack adequate nutrition due to limited availability of culturally appropriate food options, negatively impacting their energy levels and well-being.

Strategies to Address Cultural Diversity Challenges

1. Implementing Multilingual Training Programs

Organizations must offer training programs in multiple languages tailored to employees' linguistic needs. These programs can include instructional videos, written materials, and workshops in diverse languages to ensure full comprehension of health and safety procedures.

2. Celebrating Diversity to Foster Inclusion

By organizing cultural days or collaborative events, companies can enhance communication among employees from different backgrounds, boosting morale and fostering teamwork.

3. Providing Culturally Diverse Food Options

Workplaces should offer varied meal options that align with employees' cultural dietary habits. This ensures adequate nutrition, supports overall health, and maintains energy levels for optimal performance.

Key Insight:

Cultural diversity in the UAE's workforce demands adaptive strategies to harmonize health and safety practices with employees' unique needs. By embracing inclusiveness through multilingual communication, cultural awareness, and tailored nutrition, organizations can create healthier, more cohesive work environments.

Third: Opportunities for Development in Occupational Health in the UAE

Despite the unique challenges facing occupational health in the UAE, there are significant opportunities to leverage these conditions to drive organizations toward improving work environments and enhancing employee safety and well-being. These opportunities include:

1. Innovation in Health and Safety Technology:

The UAE provides a fertile ground for implementing cutting-edge health and safety technologies, such as smart devices to monitor employees' body temperature and fatigue levels, and sensor systems for hazard detection. These technologies help organizations apply high safety standards and ensure rapid emergency response.

2. Developing Specialized Health Awareness Programs:

Organizations can offer tailored awareness programs that address employees' diverse cultural and health needs, such as educating them about heat stress risks and providing health tips aligned with their cultural backgrounds. These programs help build an inclusive health culture for all employees, regardless of their background.

3. Collaboration   with   Government   Entities   and Educational Institutions:

Organizations can partner with government bodies and educational institutions to develop accredited occupational health and safety training programs. This collaboration enhances workers' health and safety skills and raises awareness of the importance of occupational health.

4. Launching Culturally Inclusive Mental Health Initiatives:

Given the cultural diversity, organizations can launch mental health initiatives that account for cultural differences. This includes providing multilingual psychological counseling and support programs tailored to employees' diverse needs.

Fourth: The Role of the Government in Supporting Occupational Health

The UAE government recognizes the importance of providing healthy and safe work environments and supports public and private sector institutions in developing occupational health programs through various initiatives and legislation. Key efforts include:

1. Enforcing Strict Occupational Safety and Health Legislation:

The UAE government imposes rigorous laws related to occupational health and safety, mandating companies to adhere to the highest safety standards. These regulations aim to protect workers and promote secure work environments.

2. The Abu Dhabi Occupational Safety and Health Initiative (OSHAD):

The Abu Dhabi government launched this initiative to enhance occupational safety and health standards in the emirate. OSHAD is one of the most critical programs helping organizations develop and effectively implement safety policies.

3. Collaboration with International Institutions:

The UAE seeks to leverage global expertise in occupational health by partnering with international organizations such as the International Labour Organization (ILO). This collaboration aims to adopt the best practices and align work environments with international standards.

The UAE's climatic challenges and cultural diversity demand tailored strategies to improve occupational health and ensure employee safety and well-being. By adopting advanced programs and technologies and developing initiatives that align with work nature and diverse employee needs, the UAE offers significant opportunities for innovation and advancement in occupational health. This approach reflects the nation's commitment to sustainable development and establishing a model for healthy, safe workplaces-supporting economic growth and enhancing societal well-being as a whole.

Continuous Training and Education in Occupational Health in the UAE

Continuous training and education in occupational health play a pivotal role in creating safe and sustainable workplaces, enhancing productivity, and ensuring employee well-being. In the UAE, government and private institutions actively develop programs to meet evolving occupational safety standards. This chapter explores current efforts, challenges, and solutions to strengthen occupational health training in the UAE.

I. Importance of Occupational Health Training

Training programs are integral to workplace safety strategies in the UAE. They contribute to:

Improved Employee Safety: Equipping workers with skills to handle risks like chemical exposure or accidents.

Enhanced Productivity: Reducing workplace injuries lowers costs and boosts efficiency.

Compliance with Global Standards: Programs align with certifications like ISO 45001, enhancing institutional credibility.

Mental Health Awareness: Training addresses stress management and work-life balance, fostering healthier workplaces

II. Current Occupational Health Training Programs

The UAE government and institutions have launched several initiatives:

1. **Emirates Health Services (EHS) Clinical Training**
- Offers specialized courses in first aid, risk management, and emergency response for healthcare workers.
- Includes the Return-to-Work Program for professionals re-entering clinical practice after a hiatus, requiring continuous professional development (CPD) hours and clinical retraining.

2. **Abu Dhabi's Occupational Safety and Health Initiative (OSHAD)**
- A federal program enforcing strict safety standards and providing accredited training for healthcare and industrial sectors.

3. **Waterfalls Platform**
- A global initiative by the UAE's Ministry of Possibilities, offering remote medical training in Arabic and English for 1 million healthcare professionals worldwide.

4. **Digital Academy**
- Provides free online courses in cybersecurity, business management, and AI, accessible to federal employees and private-sector workers.

5. **National Occupational Safety and Health Program**
- Accredited training for roles like "Occupational Health Specialist" and "Safety Officer," with exams and e-portfolios to ensure competency

III. Challenges in Implementing Training Programs

Despite the great progress in the development of training and education programs in occupational health, there are challenges facing the effective implementation of these programs, the most prominent of which are:

1. Cultural and Linguistic Diversity

A multilingual workforce requires training materials in multiple languages, complicating communication.

2. Harsh Climate

Extreme heat limits outdoor training effectiveness, necessitating adjusted schedules.

3. Cost and Resource Constraints

Advanced technologies like VR simulations or sensor-based systems increase expenses, challenging smaller organizations.

4. Continuous Compliance

Sectors like healthcare mandate ongoing CPD hours, adding pressure on employees to balance training with work

IV. Solutions to Enhance Training Effectiveness

To enhance the effectiveness of training and continuing education programs in the field of occupational health, a set of solutions and strategies can be adopted that contribute to improving the training environment and meeting the needs of workers

1. Multilingual and Culturally Adapted Programs

Example: The Waterfalls platform offers Arabic and English courses, while OSHAD mandates tailored content for diverse sectors.

2. Technology-Driven Training

Digital Academy and Mahratta platform use e-learning to deliver flexible, scalable programs.

Virtual reality (VR) simulations for hazard management training 8.

3. Partnerships with Educational Institutions

Collaboration with universities like the University of Sharjah to develop accredited occupational health curricula.

4. Climate-Adapted Scheduling

Midday work bans (12:30 PM–3:00 PM) during summer reduce heat exposure, aligning with training schedules.

5. Cost-Effective Models

Million Coders Initiative provides free coding and AI training, reducing financial barriers

V. Global examples and lessons learned and UAE's Progress

1. Singapore's Simulation-Based Training

UAE adopts VR and AI-driven modules, similar to Singapore's advanced hazard simulations.

2. UK's Multilingual Frameworks

Inspired by the UK, UAE institutions like Waterfalls offer courses in Arabic and English to bridge language gaps.

3. OSHA-Inspired Sector-Specific Programs

UAE's OSHAD mirrors the U.S. OSHA model, targeting risks in energy, construction, and healthcare

Hints

The UAE's commitment to occupational health training is evident through initiatives like OSHAD, Waterfalls, and the Digital Academy. While challenges like linguistic diversity and climate persist, solutions such as multilingual e-learning and partnerships with global institutions position the UAE as a leader in sustainable workplace safety. By integrating technology and best international practices, the UAE advances toward its vision of becoming a global model for occupational health

The Importance of Collaboration in Education and Training Programs in the UAE

Education and training programs in occupational health, along with cross-sector collaboration, form a cornerstone of the UAE's strategy to enhance safe and healthy workplaces. These programs play a vital role in improving employee performance, reducing accidents, and developing skills aligned with the highest health and safety standards. Achieving these goals requires unified efforts across government entities, the private sector, and educational institutions to deliver effective training and support sustainable development in occupational health.

First: Importance of Occupational Health Education and Training

Education and training programs in occupational health are fundamental to building safe and efficient workplaces. Their significance lies in:

1.   **Enhancing Employee Safety:** Training equips employees to identify and address workplace hazards, reducing accidents and injuries.

2.   **Boosting Efficiency and Productivity:** Providing employees with knowledge and skills improves their performance and productivity.

3.   **Compliance with Local and International Standards:** Programs ensure adherence to standards like ISO, enhancing

institutional reputation and stakeholder trust.

4. **Achieving Workplace Sustainability:** Fostering a safety-oriented culture reduces accident-related costs and promotes long-term sustainability.

Second: Current Occupational Health Education and Training Programs in the UAE

The UAE government has launched several initiatives focused on occupational health education and training:

1. **National Training Initiatives:**

The National Occupational Health and Safety Training Program equips workers in healthcare and industrial sectors with risk management and safety skills.

2. **Abu Dhabi Health Department Programs:**

Offers courses in first aid, crisis management, and environmental safety for healthcare professionals.

3. **Dubai Health Authority's Medical Specialization Program:**

Trains doctors and healthcare practitioners use real-world simulations to enhance emergency response capabilities.

4. **Industrial and Construction Sector Training:**

The Ministry of Human Resources and Emiratization provides multilingual courses for sectors like oil, gas, and construction, covering chemical handling, fall protection, and fire safety.

Third: Cross-Sector Collaboration to Strengthen Occupational Health

Partnerships between government, private, and academic sectors are critical to advancing occupational health:

1. **Government-Private Sector Collaboration:**

Joint programs like those by the Ministry of Human Resources and major construction/energy companies ensure compliance with safety standards.

2. **Academic Partnerships:**

Universities and technical institutes integrate occupational health into curricula, offering specialized courses and internships.

3. **International Cooperation:**

Collaboration with organizations like the International Labour Organization (ILO) and OSHA promotes the best global practices of globalization.

4. **Insurance Sector Engagement:**

Partnerships with insurers help companies manage risks and reduce insurance costs through tailored safety programs.

Fourth: Challenges in Occupational Health Training

1. **Cultural and Linguistic Diversity:** Requires multilingual training materials and culturally adapted content.

2. **High Costs:** Advanced programs with VR simulations or sensor technologies strain budgets for smaller firms.

3. **Varying Awareness Levels:** Some sectors lag in prioritizing occupational health, necessitating targeted awareness campaigns.

V. Solutions to Enhance Training Effectiveness

1. **E-Learning Platforms:** Interactive online courses with simulations and quizzes for flexible learning.

2. **Global Partnerships:** Collaborate with multinational firms to adopt international best practices.

3. **Government Grants:** Financial incentives for SMEs to invest in advanced training.

4. **Academic Integration:** Universities and companies co-develop accredited occupational health certifications.

5. **Virtual Reality (VR) Training:** Adopt Canada's VR-based hazard simulations for high-risk sectors like construction.

Fifth: Proposed solutions to enhance the effectiveness of education and training programs

Occupational health education and training programs can be improved by:

Develop online and interactive training programs: Online platforms help provide training content that is available to everyone at any time, allowing employees to access training programs easily. These platforms can include recorded lectures, interactive quizzes, and practice simulation games.

Collaborate with multinational companies to develop global content: The UAE can benefit from the expertise of international companies in developing training programs based on the best international practices, and continuously updating curricula to keep pace with rapid changes in the industry.

Provide government grants to support training: The government can provide financial grants or tax deductions to companies that invest in occupational health and safety training, incentivizing SMEs to implement advanced training programs.

Strengthening partnerships with academic institutions: Government institutions and private companies can collaborate with universities and technical institutes to provide advanced training courses in the field of occupational health and safety and provide students with practical training opportunities within institutions.

Provide accredited certificates in occupational health: Accredited professional certificates contribute to encouraging employees to develop and make progress in the field of occupational health. The UAE can collaborate with international accreditation bodies to provide internationally recognized certifications in areas such as environmental safety management and public health.

Sixth: Successful global models and lessons learned

1. **Singapore's Collaborative Model:** Integrates government, private, and academic sectors to deliver interactive training.
2. **Sweden's Early Education Integration:** Embeds occupational health in school curricula to foster lifelong safety awareness.
3. **Canada's VR Training:** Simulates high-risk scenarios for safer on-site preparedness.

Conclusion

The UAE's commitment to occupational health education and cross-sector collaboration underscores its vision to become a global model for safe and sustainable workplaces. By leveraging technology, international partnerships, and academic integration, the UAE enhances employee well-being and strengthens its position as a hub for innovation and investment. These efforts align with the nation's goals of economic sustainability and social prosperity, ensuring a healthier future for its workforce.

Promote health and safety in the curriculum

Integrating Health and Safety into Educational Curricula

Health and safety are the cornerstone of building a strong and sustainable society. From this perspective, integrating health and safety concepts into educational curricula from early stages represents a long-term investment in future generations. Not only does it enhance students' health awareness, but it also instills core values that foster lifelong positive behaviors.

Why Start from Early Education?

1. Early Foundation of Awareness:

Young children have a high capacity to absorb new values and knowledge. Introducing health and safety concepts at this stage empowers them to build a strong foundation for their future lives.

2. Prevention Over Treatment:

Teaching children about personal hygiene, proper nutrition, and safety principles reduces health risks and injuries. Early awareness also promotes preventive behaviors, minimizing the need for later medical interventions.

3. Promoting Positive Behaviors:

Health and safety encompass not only physical aspects but also psychological and social well-being. Educating children on stress management, building healthy relationships, and respecting others fosters a positive learning and social environment.

Benefits of Integrating Health and Safety into Curricula

1. Enhancing Daily Life Skills:

Children who learn to care for their health and make informed safety decisions develop life skills that help them confidently face future challenges.

2. Creating a Conscious and Responsible Generation:

Equipping students to recognize daily risks and address them responsibly paves the way for a vigilant and accountable society.

3. Reducing Healthcare Burden on Society:

Instilling healthy habits early reduces future rates of chronic diseases and injuries, alleviating pressure on healthcare systems.

4. Improving the School Environment:

Schools that prioritize health and safety enhance student focus and academic performance, elevating the quality of education.

Examples of Health and Safety Topics in Curricula

- **Physical Health:** Importance of nutrition, physical activity, and healthy sleep.
- **Public Safety:** Emergency response, traffic rules, and home safety.
- **Mental Health:** Stress management, self-confidence, and emotional awareness.
- **Environment and Hygiene:** Environmental conservation, personal and public hygiene.

Role of Teachers and Parents

Teachers and parents play a vital role in reinforcing these concepts. Collaboration between schools and homes ensures the continuity of values and knowledge children acquire.

Conclusion

Integrating health and safety into educational curricula from an early age is not an optionality, it is essential for building a safer, healthier future. Generations raised on preventive values and health awareness will create a strong, thriving society.

Let us start today by planting these principles in our children's minds, shaping them into tomorrow's leaders who value health and safety.

Key Message:

Health and safety education is not just a lesson-it's a lifelong investment in building resilient individuals and communities.

Chapter Six

Practical Strategies to Improve Occupational Health in the UAE

Occupational health is a fundamental component of a safe and sustainable work environment, enhancing employee well-being and productivity in settings committed to the highest safety standards. The UAE's dedication to advancing occupational health programs requires embracing modern innovations, applying artificial intelligence (AI), and updating national policies to align with rapid global changes. This chapter outlines practical strategies based on global studies and experiences, proposes policy recommendations, and defines key performance indicators (KPIs) to measure the effectiveness of occupational health initiatives.

First. Innovation and Technology in Risk Analysis and AI Solutions

Advanced technologies have revolutionized occupational health, and the UAE is a pioneer in adopting innovations to improve workplaces. By leveraging AI, sensors, and virtual reality (VR), organizations can enhance safety protocols, reduce accidents, and identify risks in real time. Key digital transformation tools include:

1. Risk Analysis Using Artificial Intelligence

AI is a powerful tool for proactive risk prediction and analysis. It processes vast datasets from production processes and human performance to identify patterns and preventive solutions.

- **Big Data Analysis:** AI analyzes historical safety incident data to identify recurring risk factors. Machine learning improves systems' ability to predict incidents and develop tailored response plans.

- **Accident Prediction:** Predictive AI models prepare organizations to take preemptive measures. For example,

AI can detect abnormal machinery temperature spikes and alert maintenance teams.

Case Study – Japan: Japanese automotive factories reduced workplace accidents by 30% using AI to monitor employee behavior and correct unsafe actions.

2. Virtual Reality (VR) and Augmented Reality (AR) Technologies

VR and AR simulate hazardous environments for risk-free training, enhancing preparedness for emergencies.

- **Interactive Training:** VR immerses employees in virtual high-risk scenarios, such as construction sites or oil rigs, improving their ability to handle real-world dangers.
- **Accident Prevention:** These technologies train workers to operate heavy machinery and handle hazardous materials safely.

Case Study – Canada: VR training in construction reduced fall-related accidents by 40% by teaching balance and caution at heights.

3. Wearable Sensors and Devices

- **Health Monitoring:** Smart wearables (e.g., bracelets) track vital signs like heart rate and body temperature, detecting early signs of heat stress or fatigue.
- **Hazard Detection:** Workplace sensors identify toxic chemicals or gas leaks, enabling immediate evacuation.

Case Study – UAE Oil Sector: Gas detection sensors on drilling platforms significantly improved worker safety by predicting toxic exposure risks.

4. Robotics and Automation

- **High-Risk Task Automation:** Robots perform dangerous tasks (e.g., pipeline inspections, chemical handling), reducing human exposure to hazards.

- **Automated Inspections:** Robots conduct routine checks in hazardous areas, identifying malfunctions before they escalate.

Case Study – ADNOC: Abu Dhabi National Oil Company uses robots to inspect and clean pipelines, minimizing employee risks.

Second. Recommendations for Updating National Occupational Health Policies

To enhance occupational health, the UAE should adopt flexible, tech-driven policies:

1. Laws Promoting Technology Adoption

Incentivize companies to adopt AI and sensor technologies through tax exemptions.

Mandate robotics and smart devices in high-risk industries and train employees to use them.

2. Continuous Employee Training Policies

Require regular VR- and AI-based occupational health training.

Provide government grants to SMEs for advanced training programs.

3. Climate Adaptation Standards

Implement flexible work hours and mandatory rest breaks during summer to prevent heat stress.

Mandate protective gear and health-monitoring wearables for outdoor workers.

4. Global Collaboration

Partners with organizations like the ILO and OSHA to align UAE standards with the best global practices.

Host international workshops to share knowledge and innovations.

5. Eco-Friendly Workplace Technologies

Encourage emission-reducing technologies to improve air quality and sustainability.

Third. Performance Indicators to Measure Effectiveness

To evaluate occupational health programs, track these KPIs:

1. Preventive Performance Indicators

- **Accident/Injury Rate:** Monthly/annual tracking of workplace incidents.

- **Absenteeism Due to Health Issues:** Reduced absenteeism indicates successful safety measures.

- Avoidable Injuries: Measures of training effectiveness in accident prevention.

2. Technological Performance Indicators

- **Adoption Rate of Smart Technologies:** Reflects reliance on AI, VR, and sensors.

- **Early Warning Alerts:** Tracks sensor systems' ability to predict risks.

- **Wearable Device Engagement:** Indicates employee utilization of health-monitoring tools.

3. Mental Health and Well-Being Indicators

- **Employee Satisfaction:** Regular surveys on workplace safety and health programs.

- **Stress Levels:** Assesses mental health support effectiveness.

- **Overall Well-Being:** Tracks chronic illness rates linked to work conditions.

4. Financial Performance Indicators

- **Accident-Related Costs:** Tracks expenses from injuries and compensation.
- **ROI on Technology:** Measures productivity gains and accident reduction from tech investments.

Hints

The UAE's ambition to lead in occupational health is evident through its adoption of AI, VR, sensors, and robotics. Flexible policies, continuous training, and global collaboration will further enhance workplace safety. By rigorously measuring performance through KPIs, the UAE ensures ongoing improvements, solidifying its role as a global model for occupational health excellence.

Key Message:

Innovation, policy agility, and data-driven strategies position the UAE at the forefront of occupational health, safeguarding workers while boosting productivity and sustainability.)

Occupational Health in the UAE – Practical Examples and Recommendations to Enhance Awareness and Practical Benefits

Occupational health is a cornerstone in building safe and effective work environments that ensure employee safety and enhance productivity. With growing awareness of the importance of implementing occupational health strategies, practical examples from the UAE and leading countries highlight the benefits of adopting innovative health policies and preventive measures.

In this chapter, we review practical examples from the UAE and other nations, discuss the benefits of applying occupational health practices, and provide recommendations to raise awareness among businesses and institutions.

First: Practical Examples from the UAE and Global Leaders in Occupational Health:

1. The UAE's Experience in Enhancing Occupational Health in the Construction Sector

The construction sector is one of the most accident-prone industries due to daily risks such as falls from heights, harsh weather conditions, and exposure to heavy machinery.

- **Dubai Municipality's Health and Safety Initiative in Construction:** Dubai Municipality launched initiatives to improve working conditions and provide intensive training programs for construction workers. These programs included training on personal protective equipment (PPE) and first aid workshops. A safety points system was also implemented, requiring periodic safety assessments for construction sites.

- **Results:** These initiatives significantly reduced workplace accidents and increased safety awareness among workers. Statistics showed a 25% decrease in work-related injuries after implementation.

2. Abu Dhabi National Oil Company (ADNOC)'s Use of Technology for Occupational Safety

ADNOC is a leader in adopting occupational health strategies through advanced technologies for risk analysis and accident prevention.

- **AI and Sensor Technologies:** ADNOC uses AI and sensors to monitor worksites in real time, analyzing data to detect potential hazards. Robots are also deployed for high-risk tasks.
- **Results:** These technologies reduced accidents and improved emergency response times. Data showed a 30% decline in toxic gas-related incidents after deploying smart sensors.

3. Sweden's Occupational Health Model in Manufacturing

Sweden is a pioneer in improving work environments, particularly in the demanding manufacturing sector.

- **Mental Health and Wellness Programs:** Sweden offers comprehensive mental health support for manufacturing employees, including counseling and stress management workshops.
- **Results:** These programs boosted employee satisfaction, reduced absenteeism by 20%, and increased productivity.

4. Singapore's Virtual Reality Training in Aviation

Singapore's aviation sector uses virtual reality (VR) to train employees for emergency scenarios.

- **VR-Based Training:** Employees train in simulated emergencies like evacuations and fire management.
- **Results:** VR training improved emergency response speed, reduced errors by 35%, and boosted employee confidence.

Second: Benefits of Occupational Health Practices and Awareness:

Effective occupational health programs enhance organizational performance, employee satisfaction, and cost savings. Key benefits include:

Improved Employee Safety: Reduced workplace injuries and absenteeism.

Increased Productivity: Safe environments foster employee morale and performance.

Lower Insurance Costs: Fewer accidents reduce compensation and insurance expenses.

Enhanced Corporate Reputation: Companies prioritizing employee health attract clients and investors.

Better Mental Health: Stress reduction improves psychological well-being.

Third: Recommendations to Enhance Awareness and Implementation:

To maximize occupational health benefits, stakeholders should:

1. **Launch Awareness Campaigns:** Use social media, workshops, and seminars to highlight best practices.

2. **Integrate Occupational Health into Corporate Culture:** Embed health and safety into organizational policies.

3. **Invest in Technology:** Adopt AI, sensors, and VR for risk prediction and training.

4. **Provide Specialized Training:** Focus on hazardous material handling, PPE, and mental health.

5. **Collaborate with Government and International Bodies:** Partner with entities like the UAE Ministry of Human Resources and ILO.
6. **Track Performance Metrics:** Monitor accident rates, absenteeism, and employee satisfaction.
- Clear performance indicators should be developed and reviewed periodically to measure the effectiveness of occupational health programs. Indicators include accident rates, employee satisfaction levels, and absenteeism rates, which help to see how successful programs are and identify areas that need improvement.

Occupational health is a critical element in achieving safe and highly productive work environments. Successful examples from the UAE and other countries demonstrate the many benefits that can be reaped by adopting effective occupational health policies and measures. Investing in technology, raising awareness and adopting practical strategies based on field studies and experiences leads to enhancing the reputation of organizations and increasing employee satisfaction and productivity. This chapter is a practical guide for organizations that aspire to achieve safe and stimulating work environments in the UAE and beyond.

The Swedish Model: A Comprehensive Approach to Occupational Health

Sweden's globally recognized system combines legislation, employer-union collaboration, mental health support, and technology:

1. Comprehensive legislation and legal regulations:

The Swedish system is based on a comprehensive set of legislation and laws that set strict occupational health and safety standards. The Swedish Working Environment Authority (Arbetsmiljöverket) oversees the application of this legislation, which aims to protect employees from risks in working environments and provide safe working conditions.

- Work environment laws: Sweden has laws that oblige employers to periodically assess the work environment, identify potential risks and take measures to reduce them. The laws also require periodic reports on the working environment to be submitted to the relevant bodies to ensure compliance with the standards. - Commitment to improving the psychological work environment: Swedish legislation also includes the protection of the mental health of employees. The law obliges organizations to take measures to reduce stress at work, prevent bullying and discrimination, and ensure a supportive work environment for all.

2. **Employer-Union Partnerships:**

The Swedish system enjoys great cooperation between employers and trade unions in the field of occupational health, with unions being key players in setting health and safety standards.

- Collective bargaining: Unions are key partners in negotiating occupational health issues and play an important role in making proposals to improve the working environment and provide additional protection for employees.

- On-the-job health coordinators: The Swedish system

includes the presence of health coordinators at the workplace, who coordinate efforts between management and employees to implement health and safety programmes and provide immediate support in case of any occupational health problem.

3. Mental Health and Wellness Programs:

Sweden places great emphasis on mental health and wellness, as it is an integral part of a healthy work environment. Swedish programs include:

- Counseling sessions: Many organizations provide psychological counseling sessions to employees to help them deal with stress and stress, which enhances psychological well-being and reduces work-related mental health problems.

- Professional-personal balance programs: Sweden encourages flexible working hours and the implementation of a remote work policy, which allows employees to set flexible working hours that contribute to achieving a balance between their personal and professional lives, reducing stress and helping to enhance their overall work satisfaction.

4. Invest in occupational health training and education:

Sweden pays great attention to training and sensitizing employees on occupational health issues and considers this area to be an essential part of the professional development process.

- Specialized training programs: The Swedish government provides advanced training programs that include the safe use of equipment and machinery, chemical handling, first aid, and accident prevention measures.

- Mental Health Training: Training programs also include providing guidance to employees on how to deal with stress at work and how to deal with feelings of anxiety or stress.

5. **Adopt technology and innovation to improve the work environment:**

Sweden uses modern technology and innovations to improve working environments, relying on a range of tools and techniques that enhance safety and provide a safer working environment.

-Use of virtual reality (VR) technologies in training: Many Swedish institutions rely on virtual reality to train employees in simulated work environments, allowing them to acquire new skills without risking their security.

- Sensors: Sweden uses sensors to monitor the working environment, such as lighting, ventilation and temperature levels, ensuring a comfortable and healthy working environment.

6. **Performance Indicators and Quality Control**

Sweden is one of the countries that rely on performance indicators to measure the effectiveness of occupational health programs, where data is collected and analyzed periodically.

- Accident and injury rate monitoring: Organizations monitor accident and injury rates periodically to evaluate the performance of health and safety programs and determine the required improvement actions.

- Employee satisfaction with the work environment: Employee satisfaction rates with the work environment are one of the main indicators that Sweden relies on to assess occupational health. Satisfaction is measured through periodic questionnaires to ensure that the work environment aligns with employee expectations.

Case Studies from Sweden: Practical Applications of Occupational Health

1. Volvo Cars

Volvo relies on innovative strategies to promote occupational health within its plants. The company implements comprehensive training programs that include the use of virtual reality technologies to simulate work environments, and training employees to handle heavy machinery. Volvo also offers psychological support programmes and flexible working hours to reduce stress.

- **Results:** The company was able to reduce accident rates by 20%, and significantly increase employee satisfaction with the work environment, which contributed to improving productivity.

2. Healthcare Sector

The healthcare sector in Sweden relies on psychological support programs for healthcare providers, where psychological counselling and social support are provided to doctors and nurses. Policies are also in place to reduce working hours and increase the flexibility of work schedules.

- Results: The implementation of these policies reduced

absenteeism by 15% and improved patient care by reducing staff stress.

Benefits of the Swedish system in occupational health

The Swedish system is a global model that shows the practical benefits of applying occupational health comprehensively, and the most important of these benefits are:

1. **Improving the quality of work environments: Sweden's work environments are among the best in the world thanks to their focus on providing a healthy and safe environment, which contributes to employee satisfaction.**

2. **Mental health promotion: The Swedish system provides psychological support programs to employees, which contribute to reducing stress rates at work, and enhancing their general well-being.**

3. **Increase productivity: Occupational health and productivity are directly related, as providing healthy and comfortable work environments increases employee concentration and productivity and reduces absenteeism rates.**

4. **Sustainability: Occupational health policies help achieve the sustainability of work environments and reduce costs associated with accidents and injuries.**

Conclusion

Occupational health is critical for safe, productive workplaces. By adopting successful strategies from the UAE, Sweden, and Singapore, organizations can reduce risks, enhance productivity, and build sustainable operations. Investing in technology, awareness, and employee well-being ensures long-term success in the UAE and beyond.

Special recommendations based on the Swedish experience

The UAE can benefit from the Swedish experience in occupational health by adopting some similar policies and strategies:

1. **Strengthen mental health legislation:** Laws could be developed that require organizations to provide supportive work environments for mental health and encourage psychological support and stress management programs.

2. **Encourage cooperation between unions and employers:** Cooperation between institutions and unions can be strengthened to develop integrated health programs that reflect the needs of employees and balance the interests of all.

3. **Adopting technology in training and occupational safety:** It is possible to use virtual reality and sensors to provide practical training and simulate hazardous work environments, which contributes to enhancing employee readiness and reducing accidents.

4. Launch continuous awareness and training campaigns:

Periodic training on occupational health and safety should be provided at various job levels, with a focus on educating employees about the importance of commitment to safety.

The Swedish system can serve as a role model in the implementation of occupational health in the UAE, contributing to healthy and safe work environments that enhance the well-being and productivity of employees.

Provide comprehensive mental health support programs for employees in the manufacturing sector

The manufacturing sector is one of the main pillars of the economy, employing millions of employees who face daily challenges that may affect their mental health. Between long working hours, productivity stressors, and physical labor risks, attention to the mental health of employees becomes essential to ensure the sustainability of this vital sector and the well-being of its workforce.

Why Focus on Mental Health in the Manufacturing Sector?

Stressful Work Environment:

The manufacturing sector is characterized by constant pressure to meet production targets and daily challenges such as high noise levels, physically demanding tasks, and fear of occupational accidents. These factors contribute to chronic stress, which can lead to long-term mental health issues.

Impact on Performance and Productivity:

Poor mental health leads to decreased performance, increased absenteeism, and higher rates of workplace errors, negatively affecting the sector's overall efficiency.

Work-Life Balance:

Employees in manufacturing often struggle to balance intensive work schedules with their personal lives, exacerbating psychological stress and reducing their quality of life.

Comprehensive Mental Health Support Programs for Employees

1. Employee Counseling Sessions

Providing in-house psychological counselors: Enables employees to discuss personal and professional issues in a safe, confidential environment.

Periodic psychological assessments: Regular mental health screenings help detect potential issues early and address them before they escalate.

2. Stress Management Programs

Workshops on stress management: Teach employees relaxation techniques such as meditation and deep breathing, along with strategies to handle daily challenges effectively.

Reducing occupational stress: Improve work organization and ensure adequate rest periods during long shifts.

3. Enhancing Work-Life Balance

Flexible leave policies: Allow employees to adjust their schedules to meet personal and professional needs.

Family support programs: Provide resources like family counseling sessions or joint recreational activities to help employees balance responsibilities.

Expected Benefits of These Programs

1. **Improved Performance and Productivity:** Employees with good mental health are more focused and motivated, enhancing production quality and efficiency.
2. **Reduced Absenteeism:** Psychological support lowers stress-related absences, reducing costs for companies.
3. **Positive Work Environment:** Mental health programs foster a supportive workplace culture, boosting employee satisfaction and retention.
4. **Fewer Occupational Accidents:** Mentally healthy employees are more alert, reducing accident risks in manufacturing settings.

Implementation Strategies

- **Partner with mental health experts:** Collaborate with specialists to design tailored programs for the manufacturing sector.
- **Awareness campaigns:** Educate employees about mental health importance and self-care strategies.
- **Measure outcomes:** Evaluate program effectiveness through employee surveys and track changes in performance and absenteeism.

Supporting mental health in manufacturing is not a luxury but an investment in organizational success and employee well-being. Comprehensive programs combining counseling, stress management, and work-life balance initiatives create healthier, integrated workplaces, benefiting everyone.

A Roadmap for Enhancing Productivity and Safety

Achieving safe and productive work environments requires a clear vision and a systematic strategy, so that every occupational health worker knows their role and effective ways to improve safety and productivity. In this area, we will present a roadmap for occupational health professionals, from the essential roles to be performed, to how to measure success. We will also review the impact of applying best practices in occupational health on increasing productivity and reducing accidents.

First: Launching a roadmap for workers in occupational health

The roadmap is a practical guide that helps occupational health professionals set goals, organize roles, and achieve common goals. Here are the main steps that occupational health professionals should follow to achieve a healthy and safe work environment:

1. Risk Identification and Assessment

- Risk identification and assessment are the first steps in the roadmap for achieving occupational health. - Employees should conduct a thorough assessment of potential risks in the work environment.
- Conduct preliminary risk assessments (e.g., machinery accidents, chemical exposure).
- Use AI and sensors for real-time hazard detection and predictive analytics.

2. Action Plans

Based on the results of the assessment, an action plan should be developed that focuses on preventive measures and identifies the steps to be followed to mitigate the risks.

- Prioritization: Based on the degree of risk, work is prioritized. For example, priority can be given to reducing high-risk incidents.

- Develop robust health policies: Comprehensive policies should be developed that define the responsibilities of each individual in the organization with regard to the application of occupational health, and clarify the procedures to be followed in emergency situations

3. Training and Development

Training is the cornerstone of the roadmap, where organizations must provide regular training to employees on how to deal with risks and follow occupational health standards.

- Safety training: includes specialized training in safety procedures such as first aid, the use of personal protective equipment, and the ability to handle dangerous machinery and equipment.

- Technology training: Employees should be trained to use smart technology, such as sensors, and virtual reality applications that help them identify and interact with hazardous work environments safely.

4. Promote awareness and safety culture

Occupational health professionals must have a deep understanding of the importance of promoting a safety culture in the work environment.

- Organizing awareness campaigns: Encourage awareness through regular campaigns that educate employees about safety best practices and how to maintain a safe work environment.
- Effective communication: Provide open channels of communication between the Occupational Health Department and employees to ask questions and express concerns, which promotes a culture of safety.

5. Performance monitoring and evaluation

Measuring and monitoring performance regularly helps to improve occupational health strategies and ensure their effective application.

- Use of performance indicators: such as accident rate, safety compliance rate, and attendance rate. These indicators help measure the effectiveness of the application of safety practices in the work environment. - Conduct periodic reviews: include reviews to ensure that all processes are conducted to set standards and make updates to policies and procedures as needed.

Second: The impact of applying the best practices on productivity and safety

Applying best practices in occupational health is not just a regulatory procedure, but an investment that benefits both employees and organizations. Here are some of the positive effects that can be achieved by applying the best occupational health practices:

1. Improve productivity and enhance performance

- Increased focus and efficiency: Employees feel safe in work environments that support occupational health, increasing their focus and ability to work efficiently.

- Reducing the rate of absenteeism: When applying healthy practices, absenteeism rates due to injuries or stress decrease, which reflects positively on work continuity and increased productivity.

2. Reduce accidents and injuries in the work environment

- Provide a safe environment: Preventive measures help reduce the rate of accidents, through the adoption of early warning techniques and the provision of personal protective equipment.

- Immediate risk management: Real-time monitoring of workplaces allows detection of any changes that may pose a risk to employees and rapid intervention, reducing the likelihood of accidents.

3. Achieving the sustainability of the work environment

- Reduce costs associated with compensation: Reducing the accident rate reduces the costs incurred by organizations to pay injury compensation, preserving the organization's budget and achieving financial sustainability.

- Enhancing business continuity: Organizations that adopt the best occupational health practices have a greater ability to meet challenges and maintain business continuity, which achieves greater flexibility and reliability in performance.

4. Improve the reputation and attractiveness of the organization to customers and employees

- Building trust with customers: Organizations that

care about the health and safety of their employees enhance their reputation in front of customers, which reflects positively on the level of trust and loyalty. - Increase the attractiveness of the organization as a workplace: Safe work environments are more attractive to current and future employees, as they want to work in an organization that provides them with a safe and supportive environment, which contributes to attracting and retaining competencies.

Case studies from the UAE and leading countries in applying best practices

1. UAE Case Study - Abu Dhabi National Oil Company (ADNOC)

ADNOC has implemented smart AI-based systems to identify hazards at worksites, such as monitoring gas levels and toxic chemicals. The company also provides safety training programs on a regular basis.

- Results: The application of these technologies has led to a significant reduction in the rate of accidents, raising awareness among employees about the importance of following safety procedures, which have increased productivity and the safety of the work environment.

2. Case study from Sweden - Volvo's safety System

Volvo relies on comprehensive occupational health programmes that include ongoing safety training and the use of virtual reality technologies in training, as well as a flexible policy that supports the mental health of employees.

- Results: These strategies contributed to reducing the accident rate and improving the level of employee satisfaction, which increased production efficiency and contributed to improving the overall work environment

3 Case Study from the United States – IBM

IBM relies on comprehensive employee safety awareness and training programs, as well as psychological counseling to reduce stress levels at work.

- Results: This led to a reduction in absenteeism, improved employee performance and increased satisfaction, which positively affected the quality of production and services.

Recommendations to promote the best practices in occupational health

1. Adopt real-time risk analysis technologies (AI, sensors).
2. Develop interactive VR training programs.
3. Clarify roles and update occupational health policies regularly.
4. Track KPIs (accident rates, employee satisfaction).
5. **Promote mental health support and adequate rest periods.**

By prioritizing occupational and mental health, manufacturing sectors can achieve excellence, ensuring happier, more productive employees and sustainable organizational success.

Chapter Seven

Innovation and Automation in the UAE: Towards Integrated Sustainability in Work Environments

The United Arab Emirates (UAE) is witnessing remarkable advancements in innovation and automation, positioning itself as a global leader in enhancing occupational health through the adoption of cutting-edge technologies. In this chapter, we conclude the book by highlighting the UAE's approach to leveraging technology and innovation to create healthy and safe work environments. We also present key recommendations for achieving sustainable occupational health across industries.

First: The UAE's approach to innovation and automation to promote occupational health

The UAE places significant emphasis on deploying the latest technologies to improve occupational health. Its efforts are evident in developing advanced infrastructure that supports smart technologies and fosters a sustainable safety culture in the workplaces. The UAE's approach can be summarized as follows:

1. Use AI for risk analysis and safety monitoring

AI technologies have become integral to the UAE's occupational systems, enabling proactive risk analysis and prevention.

- Big Data Analysis: Major UAE companies, such as ADNOC, rely on big data analytics to identify hazardous patterns in workplaces. AI empowers companies to monitor safety levels proactively.

- Real-Time Monitoring: AI-connected sensors detect unexpected changes in work environments-such as chemical leaks or elevated noise levels-enhancing rapid response from safety teams.

2. Virtual Reality (VR) in Occupational Training

The UAE is a pioneer in adopting VR for employee training, simulating high-risk environments to prepare workers without exposing them to danger.

- **Emergency Scenario Training:** VR offers interactive simulations for emergencies like fires or chemical spills, boosting employee competence and reducing accidents.
- **Continuous Training and Evaluation:** VR enables ongoing training and assessment, ensuring employees remain prepared for emergencies.

3. Robotics in High-Risk Tasks

UAE companies deploy robots for hazardous tasks, particularly in industries like oil, gas, and construction.

- Automated Inspection and Maintenance: Robots inspect hard-to-reach or dangerous areas, such as pipelines and oil rigs.
- **Enhanced Safety and Reduced Human Risk:** Robotics minimize direct human exposure to dangerous equipment, reducing accidents and ensuring safer workplaces.

4. Smart Applications for Mental Health and Wellness

UAE organizations offer smart apps to help employees monitor their mental and physical health, promoting overall wellbeing.

- **Digital Mental Health Consultations:** Apps provide psychological counseling, reducing stress and improving mental health.
- **Regular Health Tracking:** These apps track biometrics like physical activity and stress levels, fostering healthier lifestyles.

Second: Recommendations for Achieving Sustainable Occupational Health Across Industries

To ensure comprehensive occupational health sustainability, the UAE should implement strategies that prioritize safe and healthy work environments. Key recommendations include:

1. **Encouraging Investment in Innovation and Technology**

- **Support R&D:** Organizations should fund research programs to develop new safety technologies, partnering with universities and research institutes.
- **Invest in Smart Devices:** Deploy AI sensors across workplaces to monitor risks and analyze real-time data, enabling accident prediction and prevention.

2. **Promote Continuous Education and Training**

- **Interactive Training Programs:** Implement tech-driven training using virtual reality VR and augmented reality (AR) to equip employees with risk management skills.
- **Mental Health Training:** Offer programs to help employees manage stress, improving performance and reducing absenteeism.

3. **Promoting a Culture of Safety and Sustainability**

- **Awareness Campaigns:** Launch regular campaigns to embed occupational health into daily routines.
- **Employee Involvement:** Engage employees in health policy decisions to foster accountability and compliance.

4. **Developing Performance Metrics to Measure Success**

- **Regular Impact Assessments:** Use metrics like accident rates and employee satisfaction to evaluate occupational health programs.

- Policy Reviews: Conduct periodic reviews to align policies with global advancements and sustainability goals.

5. Encouraging Eco-Friendly Work Environments

- Green Technologies: Invest in eco-friendly solutions like advanced ventilation and air recycling systems.
- Sustainability Initiatives: Promote green practices, such as carpooling and reducing non-renewable resource use.

The Path to a Sustainable Future for Occupational Health in the UAE

Occupational health is central to the UAE's long-term sustainability plans, enhancing workplace environments and attracting global talent. By adopting advanced innovation and automation, the UAE sets a global benchmark for occupational health policies that prioritize employee wellbeing and productivity.

The UAE's vision transforms workplaces into sustainable ecosystems through smart technology, psychological support, and interactive training, improving employees' quality of life. Clear roadmaps and globally informed recommendations position the UAE as a leader in occupational health, reducing workplace accidents and boosting productivity.

The Future of Occupational Health in the UAE
Focus on Wellbeing, Health, and Safety in Workplaces

With rapid innovation, occupational health remains a cornerstone of the UAE's strategy to provide safe, healthy workplaces that enhance productivity. The UAE's future vision aligns with its leadership's commitment to human-centric development.

First: The importance of well-being in future Workplaces

Wellbeing drives employee satisfaction and productivity, encompassing mental, physical, and holistic health. Benefits include:

- **Increase productivity and performance:**

Well-being-focused work environments support employee engagement and productivity, where employees feel valued and that their health and safety are part of the company's investment in them.

- **Reducing stress and job stress:**

Paying attention to mental health and providing flexible environments contribute to reducing job stress rates, which reflects positively on the overall health of employees.

- **Talent Attraction and Retention:**

Organizations that care about the safety and well-being of their employees are more attractive to talent, as individuals want to work in environments that value their health and seek their well-being.

- **Innovation and creativity:**

Supportive work environments provide a relaxed and stimulating atmosphere that helps employees focus and create where employees can bring their best ideas and experiences.

Second: The UAE government's Commitment and keenness to achieve well-being, health and safety

The UAE government gives the highest priority on the welfare of society, including the well-being and health of employees and workers in various sectors. The UAE has developed several national policies and programs aimed at improving the quality of life in work environments, and this interest has been reflected in innovative strategic plans and programs.

- **National Occupational Health Strategies:**
- **Occupational Health Strategy:** The Government is developing integrated strategies aimed at improving occupational health and safety, including strict safety standards and a comprehensive manual for preventive measures at work sites.
- **Mental Health and Wellness Legislation:** UAE legislation includes mental health and wellness requirements, where companies must provide stress-free work environments and stimulate wellness initiatives such as psychological counseling sessions and stress management programs.
- **Government Initiatives Supporting Employee Wellbeing**
- **Happiness and Positivity at Work Program:** The UAE government has launched national initiatives for happiness and positivity in work environments, aimed at enhancing employee satisfaction and creating inspiring work environments. This program consists in providing courses and training programs to raise the level of happiness at work.

- Annual Competitions for the Best Work Environment: The UAE government supports the organization of annual competitions to select the best work environments in the fields of occupational health and safety. These competitions encourage organizations to adopt the best practices of occupational welfare and health and enhance competitiveness in this field.

- Technology-Driven Occupational Health

The UAE seeks to take advantage of modern technology to enhance work environments, as technical innovation is one of the essential tools to improve occupational health. The techniques used include:

- **AI for data analysis and risk forecasting:** AI helps analyze data related to incidents and make predictions about future risks, enabling proactive action to protect employees.

- **Virtual reality training:** Virtual reality technologies are used to train employees in hazardous work environments in a simulated manner, providing safe environments for training and enhancing their ability to deal with risks.

- **Smart Employee Health Monitoring Apps:** Smart apps provide tools for employees to monitor their health status and track stress levels, helping to enhance their well-being and enabling stakeholders to provide immediate support when needed.

- Partnerships with the private sector and international institutions.

- **Cooperation with international institutions:** The UAE

cooperates with international organizations such as the International Labor Organization (ILO) and the US Occupational Safety and Health Agency (OSHA) to achieve the highest standards in occupational health and adopt international best practices.

- **Partnership with leading companies:** The UAE government encourages public-private partnerships to improve occupational health practices, working with leading companies to develop training programs and implement advanced safety standards.

Third: Recommendations for Enhancing Future Sustainability of occupational health

In order to achieve long-term sustainability of occupational health in the UAE, recommendations should be adopted to ensure the continuity of well-being and safety in the workplace:

1. Regular Policy Updates

- **Review legislation regularly:** It is advisable to regularly update national legislation to suit labor market developments, and to ensure compatibility with the latest developments and challenges

- **Include mental wellbeing requirements:** Ensure that national policies include clear requirements to support mental health and wellness in work environments.

2. Investment in Smart Technologies

- **Artificial intelligence and predictive analysis:** It is recommended to expand the use of artificial intelligence in monitoring and analyzing occupational health data, which helps in predicting risks and enhancing safety.

- **Training using advanced technology:** The use of technologies such as virtual reality and augmented reality in employee training should be promoted, especially in high-risk sectors.

3. Fostering a Culture of Occupational Health

- **Regular employee training:** Provide ongoing health and safety training programs, and provide awareness content on the importance of well-being, which enhances the safety culture of employees.

- **Encouraging staff participation:** Support staff participation in health policy development through periodic meetings and questionnaires, increasing their commitment to occupational health practices.

4. Develop indicators to measure the effectiveness of occupational health programs

- **Use key performance indicators:** Indicators such as accident rate, job satisfaction levels, and absenteeism rates should be identified to measure the effectiveness of occupational health programs.

- **Conduct periodic employee satisfaction surveys:** Periodic questionnaires should be submitted to assess employee satisfaction with occupational welfare and health programs, and provide improvements based on feedback.

5. Encouraging Flexible and Eco-Friendly Workplaces

- **Remote work and flexible working hours:** It is advisable to provide flexible work options where possible, especially for jobs that do not require field presence, which contributes to improving the balance between professional and personal life.

- **Use environmentally friendly technologies:** Green technologies can be used that reduce environmental impact and support the sustainability of work environments, enhancing the health and well-being of employees.

UAE Vision For a bright future in occupational health

Occupational health and wellbeing are an integral part of the UAE's vision to build a balanced and sustainable society. The UAE government's commitment to promoting healthy work environments and adopting modern technology contributes to achieving the highest standards of health and safety and makes the UAE a global role model.

The UAE's vision revolves around investing in human health and well-being, where the safety and well-being of employees is a key pillar for a thriving and sustainable economy. By implementing recommendations that include updating policies, investing in technology, and promoting a culture of safety, the UAE can reach a future where safe and stimulating work environments increase productivity and support the well-being of each individual.

Envisioning the Future:
Innovation for UAE Work Environments Reflects quality of life and embraces wellness

As the UAE confidently moves into the future, its ambition is to become a global model in quality of life and enhancing work environments. Innovation and creativity are key to establishing Emirati work environments that embrace wellness and achieve the well-being of employees, as the country focuses on adopting modern technology and artificial intelligence applications to promote occupational health and safety and create comfortable and positive work environments.

First: Envisioning the future through innovation in occupational health

The UAE looks to the future as an area for innovative solutions that enhance work environments and support the quality of life for workers. With the development of technology and the increasing reliance on artificial intelligence, there are unprecedented opportunities to improve occupational health, including monitoring the status of employees, providing real-world training, and providing flexible working environments.

1. Artificial intelligence to analyze health data and predict risks

AI represents the future of occupational health thanks to its ability to analyze huge amounts of data and identify risk patterns in work environments.

- **Predictive data analysis:** AI systems can predict potential risks based on past data, allowing proactive action to be taken to avoid accidents.
- **Provide individual solutions:** Smart technologies can provide individual health recommendations to employees based on their health status, contributing to personal wellness.

2. Virtual and augmented reality for effective training

Virtual reality and augmented reality technologies are innovative tools that enable employees to train in simulated environments, helping them meet the challenges of the work environment without being compromised.

- **Emergency Training:** Virtual reality can be used to train employees to deal with emergencies such as fires or chemical leaks, enhancing their preparedness and reducing errors.
- **Interactive and continuous training:** This technology enables continuous and up-to-date training without the need to incur high field costs, making employees always aware of the latest safety and security technologies.

3. Digital healthcare technologies to promote wellness

The mental and physical health of workers in the UAE is paramount, and the government is working to support healthy, wellness-focused work environments using digital healthcare technologies.

- **Smart Health Apps:** The UAE provides smart applications to monitor the mental and physical health of employees, helping them track their health status and obtain immediate consultations.

- **Telemedicine:** Telemedicine technologies allow employees to access health care directly in their workplaces, contributing to reducing stress, saving time and achieving holistic wellness.

Second: The UAE government's vision to establish work environments that reflect the quality of life

The UAE government places people at the heart of its vision for the future, with quality of life at the heart of its strategic plans. The UAE seeks to achieve sustainable work environments that value wellness and reflect a high quality of life, through several initiatives and programs.

- **Quality of Life Strategy**

The UAE has launched a comprehensive wellbeing strategy aimed at improving the well-being of citizens and residents, and work environments are a key part of this strategy.

- **Supporting mental health in work environments:** The strategy focuses on providing programs that support the mental health of workers and provide them with tools to balance work and personal life.

- **Encouraging flexible working methods:** Flexible working policies are part of enhancing the quality of life, with the government providing remote work options and flexible working hours to help employees achieve a healthy balance.

- **Smart Cities and Technology-Friendly Work Environments**

The UAE government seeks to transform cities into smart cities that use technology to improve the quality of life, and this vision includes providing work environments that rely on smart technology to raise the level of safety and wellness.

- **Connected work environments:** The UAE government encourages the creation of work environments that rely on smart sensors and communications to monitor working conditions and react immediately to any potential risks.

- **Stimulating innovation:** Through government initiatives, such as innovation labs and technology free zones, the country provides work environments that encourage innovation and creativity in the public and private sectors.

- **Global partnerships in occupational health promotion**

The UAE is strengthening its partnerships with international organizations to improve occupational health standards, collaborating with entities such as the International Labour Organization (ILO) and the US agency OSHA to adopt and apply international best practices in UAE work environments.

- **International conferences and workshops:** The UAE hosts international conferences and events that bring together experts and specialists in the field of occupational health, which promotes the exchange of experiences and the application of innovative solutions.

- **International Training Programs:** Through partnerships with international institutions, the UAE offers training programs based on international standards in health and safety, enhancing the skills of workers and providing a safer work environment.

Third: Establishing a culture of occupational health for the future

Sustaining work environments requires more than just policies, it needs to establish a holistic culture of occupational health among workers and employers. To achieve this vision, the UAE is moving to establish a culture of safety and wellness within institutions through education, awareness and community participation.

- **Continuing Education and Training**

The UAE government supports continuing education programs for occupational health workers, where organizations must provide periodic training that encourage innovation and safety.

- **Wellbeing awareness:** Training includes promoting awareness about personal well-being and the importance of mental and physical health care, enabling employees to better cope with work stress.

- **Innovation training:** Work environments should encourage innovation in occupational health, enhancing employees' thinking about creative solutions and developing their willingness to react to challenges.

2. Involve employees in the development of occupational health strategies

The UAE promotes a culture of engagement between employees and employers, where organizations must engage workers in developing health and safety policies and making suggestions for improving work environments.

- **Interaction with employees:** Employers can organize hearings and workshops to discuss occupational health challenges and leverage feedback to develop new policies.

-   **Stimulating community innovation:** Encouraging employees to participate in improving work environments makes them more committed to safety and promotes the spirit of innovation in finding solutions that suit their needs.

3. Promote environmental sustainability in occupational health

Environmental sustainability is an essential part of quality of life, so the UAE government encourages organizations to use technologies that reduce environmental impact and improve the work environment. -Encouraging the use of renewable energy: The government encourages the adoption of renewable energy in the operation of offices and facilities, which improves air quality and reduces the harmful effects on the health of employees.

-   **Reducing harmful emissions:** Organizations in the UAE adopt technologies that reduce emissions and pollution in the work environment, improving the overall health of workers and creating environmentally friendly work environments.

UAE Work Environments A model for quality of life and wellness

The UAE seeks to build a global model in occupational health that reflects its commitment to the well-being of its citizens and residents. Innovation is central to the UAE's strategy to establish work environments that support health and safety and reflect a high quality of life. By investing in artificial intelligence, promoting a culture of safety, and developing sustainable policies, the UAE is heading towards a bright future that highlights it as a role model.

Envisioning the future through innovation and a focus on wellbeing not only enhances the health and safety of employees but also contributes to the UAE's sustainable development and affirms its position as a global hub that embraces quality of life and values people.

Investment
In human knowledge

Investing in the minds, hearts and hands that build the future

People are the core of every success, and investing in them is the smartest and most sustainable investment. When we focus on people for the sake of man, we make a difference that goes beyond numbers and achievements, to build societies capable of creativity and development in the face of challenges. In a world where innovation is accelerating, human knowledge becomes the compass that leads us into the future. Foreseeing this future means not only adapting to what is coming but actively participating in its formulation.

Through innovation and a focus on human well-being, we are shaping a brighter world, where health and safety are not just goals, but a lifestyle that enhances the quality of every day we live.

The UAE, with its ambitious vision and inspiring journey, has proven that well-being is not just a term, but a fundamental pillar of sustainable development. Not only does it improve the health and safety of employees, but it adopts strategies that place quality of life at the heart of its position, establishing itself as a global hub that values people and embraces excellence.

It is this commitment to people that puts the UAE at the forefront of believing that real success starts from within – from investing in the minds, hearts and hands that build the future. Ultimately, when we care about human beings, we give the world a better chance to become a more compassionate, innovative and life-like place.

Sources and References

Books:

- Ramazzini, B. (2001). Diseases of Workers. Chicago: University of Chicago Press.
- Stellman, J. M. (1998). Encyclopedia of Occupational Health and Safety. Geneva: International Labour Organization Publications.

Scientific Research:

- Smith, D., & Jones, R. (2015). "The Impact of Ergonomic Interventions on Musculoskeletal Disorders." Journal of Occupational Medicine, 64(3), 157-162.
- Brown, A., & Green, B. (2020). "Heat Stress in Outdoor Workers: A Systematic Review." Journal of Occupational Health, 62(2), 89-95.

Guidelines:

- World Health Organization (WHO). (2017). Healthy Workplaces: A Global Framework. Geneva: World Health Organization.
- American Conference of Governmental Industrial Hygienists (ACGIH). (2021). Threshold Limit Values for Chemical Substances and Physical Agents.

National Standards:

- Ministry of Human Resources and Emiratization in the United Arab Emirates (MOHRE). (2020)
- Occupational Safety and Health Guidelines in the UAE.
- Occupational Safety and Health Administration (OSHA). (2021).
- Occupational Safety and Health Standards (29 CFR 1910).

Online Sources:

- Abu Dhabi Public Health Center
- https://www.adphc.gov.ae/en/Public-Health-Programs
- National Institute for Occupational Safety and Health (NIOSH)
- "Occupational Safety and Health Topics"
- https://www.cdc.gov/niosh
- International Labour Organization (ILO)
- "Occupational Safety and Health at the Workplace"
- https://www.ilo.org

Professor Dr.
Nahyan Helal

Passion for Occupational Health and Awareness

Academic and Professional Background:

Professor Dr. Nahyan Helal, a prominent figure in occupational health, holds a PhD in Occupational Health from the Faculty of Medicine at the University of Surrey, UK (2011), and a master's degree in occupational health from the same university (2006). He graduated in General Medicine and Surgery from Ovidius University in Romania (2000).

Leadership and Institutional Achievements:

- Chairman of the Board of the Global Institute for Telemedicine: Leading a global strategy to develop occupational healthcare services using advanced technology.
- **Founding Member of the First Occupational Health Committee in the GCC:** Instrumental in establishing the committee in April 2007, a pivotal step in creating a regulatory framework for occupational health in the region.
- International Advisory Role: Member of the External Advisory Group for the Telemedicine Institute in Scotland since 2011, providing innovative insights to advance occupational health globally.

Innovations and Achievements in Occupational Health:

- First Emirati to obtain licenses as a Consultant and Specialist in Occupational Medicine from the Abu Dhabi Health Department in 2006.

- Certified as a Consultant in Occupational Medicine in 2017, reflecting his academic and practical excellence.
- Awarded the title of Professor by the United Arab Emirates University.

Founding the First Occupational Health Center in the UAE:

In 2016, Professor Nahyan launched the first specialized Occupational Health and Medicine Center in the UAE through HMC Group.

Services include comprehensive pre-employment medical exams, mental health programs, sick leave management, and workshops on safety and security.

Pioneering Database:

He established a comprehensive database containing information for over 90,000 employees, covering their professional backgrounds, medical histories, and lab analyses. This data supports research and improves occupational health policies in the UAE.

International Accreditation Leadership:

HMC Group has earned international certifications from the UK, Norway, and the U.S. in occupational health fields such as maritime, aviation, oil and gas, and construction, solidifying the UAE's position as a hub for excellence in this sector.

Collaborations and Partnerships:

- **Contracts with Major Institutions:** Strategic partnerships with global entities like International SOS, as well as leading local institutions such as Emirates Transport, Abu Dhabi Ports Group, ADNOC, Dubai's Roads and Transport Authority (RTA), and others. These collaborations deliver high-quality occupational health services tailored to major organizations.

Technology and Innovation in Occupational Health:

- **Adoption of Cutting-Edge Technologies:** Partnered with HMC Infotech to develop the Smart Medical System (HIS) and Smart Occupational Health System (OHS), integrating medical devices like ECG, audiometry, and radiology with a comprehensive digital platform.
- **Automation and Digitization:** Implemented since 2016, with future plans to leverage AI and iCloud storage to enhance services.
- **Data Analysis and Decision-Making:** HMC Group provides advanced analytical tools to support policymakers with precise workforce data, including vital roles, job nature, and health status, enabling evidence-based policy development.

Societal Impact:

- **Mobile Occupational Health Clinics:** Launched mobile clinics to deliver tailored occupational health services to remote areas.
- **Enhancing Productivity and Well-being:** Focused on reducing occupational risks, absenteeism, and promoting workplace safety and health.

Through his leadership and expertise, Professor Dr. Nahyan Helal has become a driving force behind the occupational health revolution in the UAE. His achievements are not only a source of national pride but also a significant contribution to advancing global occupational health standards.

Prof. Dr. Mohammed Al-Sadiq Al-Haj Ahmed

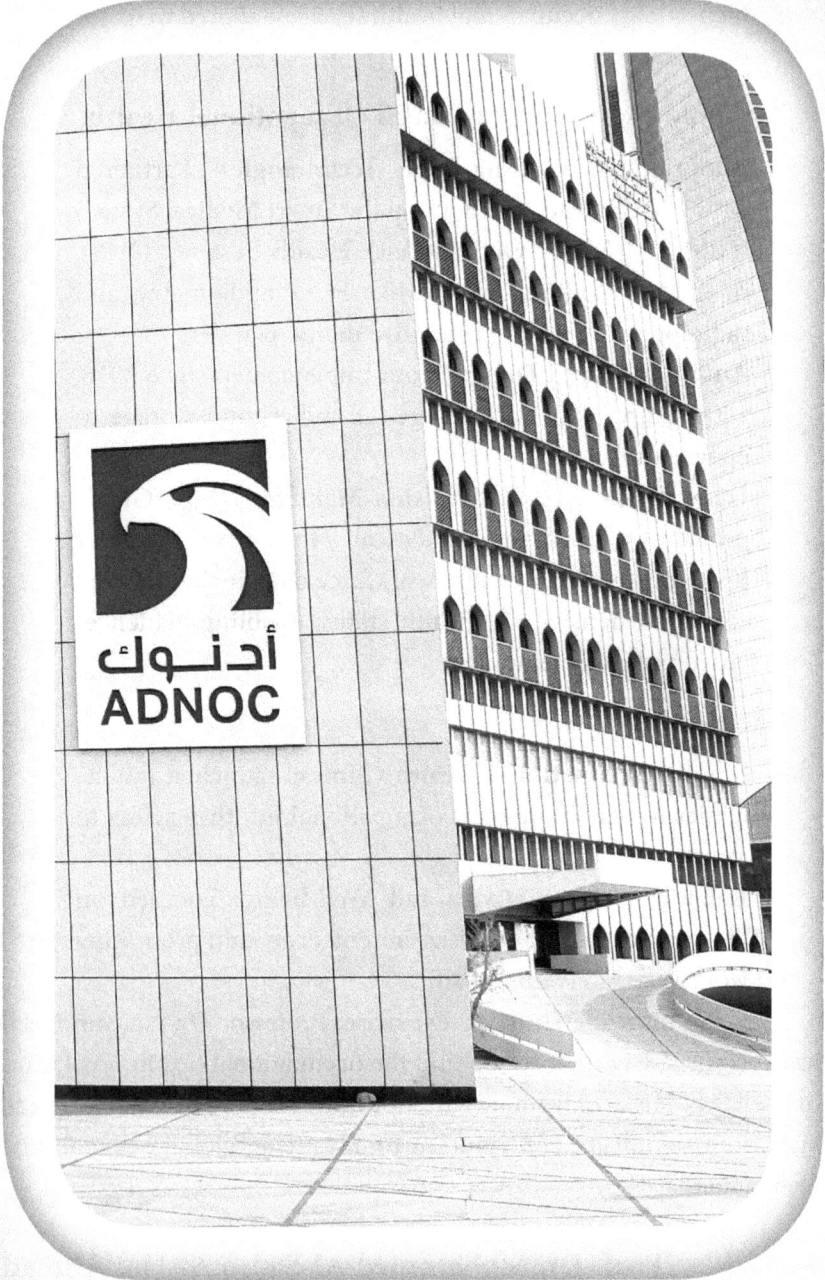

ADNOC: Innovation and Leadership in Occupational Health